Seeing the Prophet

In Dreams and Visions

First Edition: 2013
Published by: Jamiah Media
Printed and Distributed by:

Darussalam International Publications Ltd.
Leyton Business Centre
Unit-17, Etloe Road, Leyton, London, E10 7BT
Tel: 0044 208539 4885   Fax: 00442085394889
Website: www.darussalam.com
Email: info@darussalam.com

Source: bridged and summarised from Abū 'Ubaydah Mashhūr bin Hasan Āl Salmān and Abū Talhah 'Umar bin Ibrāhīm Āl 'AbdurRahmān, *al-Muqaddimāt al-Mumahhidāt as-Salafiyāt fī Tafsīr ar-Ru'yah wa'l-Manamāt* (Abu Dhabi: Maktabah Dār al-Imām Mālik, 1426 AH/2005 CE), pp.284- .

Cover design & typesetting:
www.ihsaandesign.co.uk
Edited by Abū Fātimah Azhar Majothī

SEEING THE PROPHET

In Dreams and Visions

By the Noble Shaykh
Mashhūr bin Hasan Āl Salmān
& Shaykh
'Umar bin Ibrāhīm Āl-'AbdurRahmān

Translated by 'AbdulHaq ibn Kofi ibn Kwesi al-Ashantī

DARUSSALAM

GLOBAL LEADER IN ISLAMIC BOOKS
Riyadh • Jeddah • Al-Khobar • Sharjah • Lahore • London • Houston • New York

بسم الله الرحمن الرحيم

CONTENTS

The Issue of Seeing the Prophet ﷺ in a Dream or Vision

The Messenger of Allah ﷺ said:

"Whoever sees me (in a dream or vision) has seen the truth as Shaytān does not take my form."

[THE ISSUE OF SEEING THE PROPHET ﷺ IN A DREAM OR VISION]

This theme is connected to some important issues and for that reason we viewed that we single them out for explanation and detail separately:

First Issue

———————

It has been confirmed in a number of hadīth, *sahīh* and *hasan*, that Shaytān is unable to take the form of our Prophet ﷺ, and is unable to present to the seer an image which causes him doubt as to whether it is the Prophet ﷺ or not. The most famous of these ahādīth is what has been reported by al-Bukhārī (no.6993), Muslim (no. 2266) and others from the hadīth of Abū Hurayrah ﷺ who attributed it to the Prophet (ﷺ):

> *"Whoever sees me in a dream will see me when awake, or it is as if he has seen me while awake, and Shaytān cannot resemble me."*

In al-Bukhārī (no. 6996) and Muslim (no.2267) from the hadīth of Abū Qatādah ﷺ who attributed it to the Prophet (ﷺ):

"Whoever sees me (in a vision) has definitely seen me."

And the Prophet (ﷺ) said:

"Whoever sees me (in a vision) has seen the truth as Shaytān does not take my form."

And in another narration he (ﷺ) said:

"Shaytān does not appear with my appearance."

And in yet another narration he (ﷺ) said:

"Shaytān does not take my form."

All of these narrations are authentic and most of them are found in the Two Sahīhs (al-Bukhārī and Muslim) and they clearly mean, as is apparent, that the one who sees the Prophet in a dream has really seen him and it is not an image other than that of the Prophet's ﷺ. So you should know, may Allāh honour you, that the intent of the Prophet's (ﷺ) saying: *"whoever sees me..."* means: **"sees me in my actual real form with my description and well known form at any stage of my life"**.[1] This is apparent (Mutabādir) from these

---

[1] Some 'Ulama have been narrow in this issue and have stated:

"It is a must within a vision of the Prophet ﷺ to see him in his form which he died upon. To the extent that the number of white hairs that

8

reports and their likes and this is what the Salaf ﷺ understood with its evidences and wordings, as indicated in the report of 'Awf bin Abī Jamīlah from Yazīd al-Fārisī ﷺ - and he was a scribe of the Mus-haf-, who said:

> "I saw the Prophet ﷺ in a dream during the time of Ibn 'Abbās, so I said to Ibn 'Abbās: 'I saw Allāh's Messenger ﷺ when I was asleep (i.e. in a vision).' Ibn 'Abbās said: 'Allāh's Messenger ﷺ used to say "Shaytān is unable to resemble me, so whoever sees me during sleep has definitely seen me" – so are you able to describe to me this man who you saw in your dream?' I replied: 'Yes, I describe to you a man who has a mark between his shoulders, a complexion between brown and white, black eyes, a nice smile, a beautiful round face, his beard filled between here and here (of his chest). I do not

---

he had when he died must be seen, which did not number more than twenty."

What is more correct is: that this should rather be generalised to every stage of his life with the condition that as long as it is the Prophet's actual appearance during those stages of his life whether he was young, an adult or at the end of his life. The difference of these stages could possibly be linked to the state of the one who sees the Prophet ﷺ in any of these forms and ages, and Allāh knows best. Refer to al-Hāfidh Ibn Hajar, *Fath ul-Bārī*, vol.14, p.414; Mulā 'Ali al-Qārī, *Jam' ur-Rasā'il*, vol.2, p.291; al-Haytamī al-Faqīh, *Ashraf ul-Wasā'il*, pp.596-597; al-Munāwī, *Fayd ul-Qadīr*, vol.6, p.172.

know anyone with this description.' Ibn 'Abbās said: 'If you saw him while awake you would be unable to describe him better than how you did now.'"[2]

Within this narration are great benefits; look and contemplate on the state of Ibn 'Abbās ◉ and how he mentioned a hadīth initially. He did not leave the seer of the dream until he sought clarification from him about his description and form, saying to him: **"Are you able to describe to me the man you saw?"** This shows the utmost clarity and all praise is due to Allāh. For this reason, if a man used to relate in his dream that he saw Allāh's Messenger ﷺ, the Imām of the vision interpreters from the Tābi'īn, Muhammad ibn Sīrīn ◉, would ask: **"Describe to me who you saw"** and if the person described an appearance that the Prophet was not known to have had, Ibn Sīrīn would say to the person: "you have not seen him".[3] Al-Qastalānī ◉ stated in *Irshād us-Sārī*, p.109:

---

[2] Reported by Abū Bakr bin Abī Shaybah, *al-Musannaf* (Dār ul-Fikr Print), vol.11, p.56; Imām Ahmad, *Musnad*, vol.1, pp.361-362; Ibn Sa'd, *at-Tabaqāt ul-Kubrā*, vol.1, p.417; at-Tirmidhī, *ash-Shamā'il*, vol.2, p.298; Ibn 'Asākir, *Tārīkh Dimishq* (Dār ul-Fikr), vol.14, p.121. Al-Haythamī stated in *Majma' uz-Zawā'id*, vol.8, p.272: "Reported by Ahmad and its narrators are all thiqāt."

[3] Relayed by Imām al-Bukhārī in his Sahīh, al-Hāfidh commented on this in *al-Fath*, vol.14, p.410 saying: "we narrated it with an authentic and connected chain of transmission." Our Shaykh, al-Albānī ◉, also viewed the isnad as being good within

"It is not to be considered a vision of the Prophet ﷺ except if the seer saw him in his actual appearance which he had during his life ﷺ."

The likes of this was also stated by al-Qāḍī 'Iyyāḍ in *Ikmāl ul-Mu'lim*, vol.7, p.219:

It is possible that the intent of the ḥadīth is if one sees him ﷺ with his well-known description that he had during his life. If one sees other than this then it is not a true vision and needs interpretation.[4]

Al-Bukhārī reported in *Tārīkh al-Kabīr*, vol.2, p.381, ḥadīth no.2846, as did al-Ḥākim in *al-Mustadrak*, vol.4, p.393, from 'Āsim bin Kulayb who said:

My father narrated to us: 'I said to Ibn 'Abbās: "I saw the Prophet ﷺ in a dream." Ibn 'Abbās said: "Describe

---

Hāshiyat ush-Shamā'il, p.207. He stated: "Ismā'īl al-Qāḍī narrated it from Ayyūb who said: 'Ibn Sīrīn used to...' and then he mentioned the narration." Al-'Aynī also mentioned the narration with its *isnad* and text in *Sharh al-Bukhārī*, vol.36, p.281.

[4] These words of his were transmitted by an-Nawawī in *Sharh Sahīh Muslim*, vol.15, p.25, he also transmitted from him: "it is a weak saying". A group of scholars debated this issue as mentioned in Abu'l-'Abbās al-Qurtubī, *al-Mufhim*, vol.6, p.23 and al-Qārī, *Jam' ul-Wasā'il*, vol.2, p.298 and as-Suyūtī, *ad-Dībāj*, vol.5, p.284.

him to me;" and so I described to him the appearance of Husayn bin 'Ali who resembled him, and Ibn 'Abbās said: "You have seen him."[5]

Ar-Rūyānī reported in his *Musnad*, vol.21, p.2; as did ad-Dūlābī in *al-Kunā*, vol.1, p.101; and Ibn 'Asākir in *Tārīkh Dimishq*, vol.14, p.258 – via the route of Yahyā bin Abī Bakīr: Abū Ishāq 'Ali narrated from 'Āmir bin Sa'd al-Bajalī who said:

> When al-Husayn bin 'Ali was killed I saw Allāh's Messenger ﷺ in a dream and he said: "If you see al-Barā' bin 'Āzib convey my salām to him and inform him that the killers of Husayn bin 'Ali are in the Hellfire and will face a painful torment." So I went to al-Barā' and informed him of the dream and he said: Allāh's Messenger ﷺ spoke the truth when he said: "Whoever sees me in a dream has definitely seen me as Shaytān does not take my image."[6]

Ibn Abi'd-Dunyā relayed in *al-Manāmāt*, pp.92-93 from Abū Hamza al-'Attār:

---

[5] Al-Hāfidh stated in *al-Fath*, vol.14, p.411: "The isnad is good", also refer to our Shaykh al-Albānī ﷺ in *Hāshiyat ush-Shamā'il*, p.207.

[6] Mentioned by Ibn Muflih in *Masā'ib ul-Insān* (Dār ul-'Ilmiyyah Print), p.175.

While I was with al-Hasan a man came and said: 'O Abū Sa'īd, yesterday I saw the Prophet in a vision and he said: "say to al-Hasan glad-tidings and then glad-tidings and then glad-tidings." Then tears filled al-Hasan's eyes and the man said, 'May Allāh make your eyes cool, Allāh's Messenger said: 'Whoever sees me in a dream has definitely seen me because Shaytān does not resemble my image.'"

These reports all affirm the previous acknowledgement of the necessity of seeing him ﷺ in the description which agrees with how his noble form actually was at any stage of his life.[7] Our Shaykh, al-

---

[7] [TN] In this regard I stumbled across a bizarre assertion made by Muhammad ibn Adam "al-Kawtharī" from Leicester, UK and a former student of the Deobandī Dār ul-'Ulūm in Bury, UK – he also refers to himself as a "Muftī". On the *'Sunni Path'* website in an answer to a question entitled *'How do I know that I have seen the Prophet Muhammad (Allah bless him & give him peace) in my dream?'* Muhammad ibn Adam from Leicester answered:

> The scholars have differed as to whether the dream is true in the case where one does not see the Messenger of Allah (Allah bless him & give him peace) in his recognized features and qualities, that have been transmitted in the traditions.
>
> Some scholars are of the view that the dream will only be true and genuine if the person sees the Prophet of Allah (Allah bless him & give him peace) in his recognised features. This opinion has been attributed to Qadi Iyad.

The majority of the scholars, however, including Imam Nawawi, are of the view that if a person dreams the Messenger of Allah (Allah bless him & give him peace) then his dream is true, regardless of whether he sees him on his recognized features or otherwise.

See: http://qa.sunnipath.com/issue_view.asp?HD=7&ID=1745&CATE=108

This is a very dangerous assertion which Muhammad ibn Adam al-Kawtharī brought no evidence for whatsoever and it contains the following serious errors:

1. Muhammad ibn Adam al-Kawtharī from Leicester claimed that "the 'Ulama have differed", yet not only does he fail to refer to the *Salaf*, who are the main example to follow, but he also brings no proof for such an *ikhtilāf!*

2. He claims that it is only Qādī 'Iyyād's view that one has to see the Prophet ﷺ on his recognised features, yet this is in fact the view of the companions, the Tābi'īn and those who follow them. So "Kawtharī" has used the Khalaf as the criterion and not the Salaf.

3. "Kawtharī" also claims that "the majority of the scholars" consider that a person's dream is true **"regardless of whether he sees him on his recognized features or otherwise"**. So "Kawtharī" says that this is the view of the *jamhūr* of the 'Ulama but not only does he again fail to bring any proof for this, but he also has no reflection whatsoever on the clear misguidance of such a view. This statement by Muhammad ibn Adam from Leicester is an alarming view as it necessitates that a person can see any figure within a dream who instructs him to do something and then say that it was the Prophet ﷺ because according to "Kawtharī" the figure seen in the dream does not even have to have the *recognised features or appearance* of the beloved Prophet ﷺ!!? This is the archetypal Sūfī approach which leads devils and demons to inspire them

14

Albānī ﷺ had a share in this important issue, for he stated in *as-Silsilah as-Sahīhah*,[8] after relaying a batch of *ahādīth*:

> Within these *ahādīth* it is shown that it is possible to see the Prophet ﷺ after his death even though a person may not have been a contemporary of his. However, with the condition that he sees him in his actual image during his lifetime. This is what a group of 'Ulama held as mentioned in *Fath ul-Bārī*, vol.12, p.304 – which is the saying of Ibn 'Abbās in the narration of Yazīd al-Fārisī and Kulayb the father of 'Āsim, and that of al-Barā' as has preceded. Al-Bukhārī commented on this with a report from Muhammad ibn Sīrīn, the Imām of the vision interpreters, and al-Qādī relayed it with an authentic chain of transmission from Ayyūb and said: "If a man used to relate in his dream that he saw Allāh's Messenger ﷺ the Imām of the vision interpreters from the Tābi'īn, Muhammad ibn Sīrīn ﷺ would ask: **"Describe to me who you saw"** and if the person described an appearance that the Prophet was not known to have, Ibn Sīrīn would say to the person: **"you**

---

to perform all acts of worship, and then attribute such *bātil* to the beloved Prophet ﷺ, as according to them the Prophet ﷺ *does not* even have to be seen with *his own appearance and features*!? This shows a poor understanding of *'aqīdah* issues in the guise of "traditional Islām".

[8] Vol.6, pp.513-519, hadīth no.2729.

have not seen him". Al-'Allāmah Ibn Rushd also stated in his *Fatāwā*, vol.1, pp.611-612, which was transmitted from him by al-Barzalī in his *Fatāwā*, vol.4, p.114; as did al-Wansharīsī in *al-Mi'yār ul-Mu'rib*, vol.10, p.217; and ash-Shātibī in *al-I'tisām*, vol.1, p.335:

The meaning of the Prophet ﷺ saying, "Whoever sees me has definitely seen me in truth" is that all who see him in a dream have definitely seen him in truth based on the fact that a seer may see him on different occasions in different forms. A seer could see him ﷺ in a certain description and another person could see him with another description yet it is not permissible for there to be different forms of the Prophet ﷺ or of his qualities. The hadīth rather means: whoever sees me in my appearance which I was created with has definitely seen me, because Shaytān cannot resemble me. The Prophet ﷺ did not say: "whoever thinks that he has seen me has definitely seen me."[9] Rather he said: "whoever sees me (in a dream) has definitely seen me" – as

---

[9] **[TN]** This is a superb point which the likes of Muhammad ibn Adam "al-Kawtharī" from Leicester (refer to footnote 7) need to take into consideration before making such outrageous claims like: if a person sees the Prophet then it is a true dream, "regardless of whether he sees him on his recognized features or otherwise"!

for one who thinks that he saw him yet does not know his specific image then this is not a way for anyone to know him.[10]

Al-Ḥāfidh said:

There are those who are narrow in this issue and say: "It is a must within a vision of the Prophet ﷺ to see him in his form which he died upon. To the extent that the number of white hairs that he had when he died must be seen, which did not number more than twenty." What is rather correct is: that this should instead be generalised to every stage of his life with the condition that as long as it is the

---

[10] The commentary of al-Barzalī in his *Fatāwā*, vol.4, p.114 of Ibn Rushd's words pleased me when he said:

"I say: if someone sees him ﷺ on his image which he had, as has been relayed in *ash-Shifā* and other books, the person should not take that into consideration for two reasons:

One: one has to act on decisive proof, and a vision is either opinion or doubtful and cannot be referred to in opposition to whatever is decisive let alone disregard what is decisive.

Two: a condition of a vision is precision and differentiation which is...[dependent on] the sleeper. This was noted by Ibn al-'Arabī and al-Fakhr ibn al-Khaṭīb."

Prophet's actual appearance during those stages of his life whether he was young, an adult or at the end of his life.

Shaykh 'Ali al-Qārī stated in *Sharh ush-Shamā'il*, vol.2, p.293:

It has been said that this is specific to the people of his time ﷺ, meaning "whoever sees me in a dream Allāh will bless the person to see me while awake" – yet this meaning is far from being correct...

I say[11]: I do not know of this particularisation except the hadīth of Abū Hurayrah ﷺ, found in al-Bukhārī (Sahīh, hadīth no.6993) which is attributed to the Prophet ﷺ: *"Whoever sees me in a dream will see me while awake and Shaytān does not take my form."* Al-'Aynī mentioned the meaning of this in *Sharh ul-Bukhārī*, vol.24, p.140 as being the people of the Prophet's time ﷺ: "Whoever sees him in a dream will be blessed by Allāh to make Hijrah and have the nobility of meeting him (ﷺ)." However, I doubt the accuracy of the wording *"...will see me while awake..."* because the 'Ulama of hadīth have differed over these words. Al-Bukhārī reported this but Muslim in his *Sahīh*,

---

[11] [TN] i.e. Imām al-Albānī ﷺ.

vol.7, p.54 relayed instead the words: *"...it will be as if he has seen me while awake..."* thus there is the doubt. Al-Ḥāfidh stated in *al-Fatḥ*, vol.12, p.383:

> In the narration via the route of Ismāʿīl which has been mentioned: "...has definitely seen me while awake..." and he changed the word "...will see me..." as is in the ḥadīth of Ibn Masʿūd within Ibn Mājah which at-Tirmidhī and Ibn 'Awānah authenticated. In Ibn Mājah from the ḥadīth of Abū Juhayfah "...it is as if he has seen me while awake..." this has three wordings: "...will see me while awake..."; "...it is as if he has seen me while awake" and "...has definitely seen me while awake..."

All of these verify the truthfulness of visions and the second wording is most authentic in terms of the meaning.

The intent after this explanation is that if the servant (of Allāh) sees the Prophet (ﷺ) in a dream then one should not rush to affirm this until the characteristics of who was seen is compared with the characteristics of the Prophet (ﷺ) at any stage of his life.[12] If there is agreement then the person has definitely seen him (ﷺ), yet if there is a congruence then the dream was just a muddled-up dream. Or the meaning of the dream can be the weak *īmān* of the seer and an explanation of his opposition to the Sunnah or any other meaning as deemed suitable by the vision interpreter as it relates to the seer. For this reason, Muhammad bin Abī Hamza stated:

Whoever sees him (ﷺ) with a good appearance then this symbolises the good *deen* of the seer. Yet if he is seen with a wound or the likes then this symbolises the deficiency in the *deen* of the seer, and this is true.[13]

---

[12] [TN] another point to take in consideration in light of the ridiculous view expressed by Muhammad ibn Adam al-Kawtharī from Leicester which has been discussed in the footnotes prior.

[13] *Fath ul-Bārī*, vol.14, p.413 and the likes of this was stated by al-Qarāfī in *al-Furūq* (Dār ul-'Ilmiyyah Print), vol.4, pp.414-415; also see *al-Manāmāt Bayna Ādāb ur-Rā'ī wa Qānūn il-Mu'abbir*, pp.164-165.

Second Issue

Seeing the Prophet ﷺ in a dream is not specified to only the companions (ؓ) who were his contemporaries, as opposed to the view that is held by some 'Ulama as al-'Aynī and others have transmitted. There is no evidence for this view and it opposes some narrations from the *Salaf* such as that of Ibn 'Abbās ؓ and Ibn Sīrīn ؓ. The answer of our Shaykh, al-Albānī ؓ, is a refutation of this view and all praise is due to Allāh. Some other scholars have restricted seeing the Prophet ﷺ[14] to two types of men:

> One: a companion who saw him and his image became ingrained in his soul, who would know him if he were to see him in a vision or dream.

> Two: a man who often hears about the description of the Prophet ﷺ as transmitted by books, this gets ingrained in his soul so that if he sees him ﷺ in a dream then he has seen him just as the companion would have.[15]

---

[14] Meaning: a true vision which confirms the Prophet's saying "...has definitely seen me..."

[15] Mentioned by al-Qarāfī ؓ in *al-Furūq*, vol.4, p.415

What is correct is what has been mentioned prior about visions not being restricted to anyone, rather the 'Ulama have deemed it possible and allowed for sinners, the disobedient and disbelievers to have a visions of the Prophet ﷺ which require interpretation. These can be good or bad for the seer based on the state of the seer and his vision and Allāh knows best.

Third Issue

The people of knowledge from the vision interpreters and others say: It is inappropriate for the one who sees the Prophet ﷺ in a vision to downplay the vision because it can either be glad-tidings of good or a warning from evil to scare the seer or admonish him, or possibly to even bring something to his attention about something that will happen in his *deen* or *dunyā*.[16]

They also say: Whoever sees Allāh's Messenger ﷺ in a dream then the person has seen much good. Even if he sees him within a house then this signifies that the house will be filled with good and blessings... such visions are always glad-tidings for those who see them and can symbolise for example that the person will die on Islām and be joined with the Prophet ﷺ at the Hawd and in the Paradise of ar-Rahmān (the Most Beneficent).[17]

For this reason, Abū Sa'd Ahmad bin Muhammad bin Nasr ﷺ stated:

---

[16] *Fath ul-Bārī* (Dār ul-Fikr Print), vol.14, p.413; al-Haytamī, *Asharf ul-Wasā'il*, p.596

[17] *Fath ul-Bārī*, vol.14, p.412; *Fayd ul-Qadīr*, vol.6, p.170-171; *Ashraf ul-Wasā'il*, p.596

Whoever sees a Prophet in his actual shape and form then this indicates the righteousness of the seer and his elevated status and his triumph over his enemies. Whoever sees him in a different stern looking form for example then that signifies the corrupt state of the seer, and Allāh knows best.[18]

Ibn Qutaybah ﷻ stated in *Ta'bīr ur-Ru'yah*, p.91 (our edit):

If the Prophet ﷺ is seen in a barren land it symbolises that the people of that land will be abundant. If he is seen with oppressed people it symbolises that they will be aided and if he is seen with people who are going through adversity it symbolises that they will be freed from that hardship.

In *Sharh us-Sunnah*, vol.12, p.228 of al-Baghawī it is mentioned:

If the Prophet ﷺ is seen in a vision as being in a place then that symbolises an opening for the people of that place if they are going through some adversity and restriction, and it symbolises victory if they are being oppressed.

Abū Sa'd al-Wā'idh stated in *Tafsīr ul-Ahlām*, p.21:

---

[18] *Fath ul-Bārī*, vol.14, p.415; *al-Mawāhib ul-Laduniyyah*, vol.2, p.665; *Jam' ul-Wasā'il*, vol.2, p.296; *Asharf ul-Wasā'il*, p.596; *Fayd ul-Qadir*, vol.6, p.170; at-Tuwayjurī, *Kitāb ur-Ru'yah*, p.46.

Allāh sent Muhammad (ﷺ) as a mercy to the worlds and Tūbah (a tree in Paradise) is for those who saw him during his life and followed him and Tūbah is for those who see him in dreams. If a sick person sees him then Allāh will cure the person and if a fighter sees him he will be given victory.

Fourth Issue

Many of the Mutasawwifah (Sūfīs) and people of innovation claim that they see Allāh's Messenger ﷺ while awake just as they (allegedly) see him in dreams. They also claim that he really comes out of his grave and attends their gatherings of Samā' and dancing which they call a "Hadra" which in itself means the "Hudūr" (presence) of Muhammad ﷺ. They thus transmit from their Shaykhs many things in regards to this and ascribe to Shaykh 'AbdulQādir al-Jīlānī that he was asked: **"How many times have you seen Allāh's Messenger ﷺ in a dream?"** And he allegedly replied: **"Some seventy odd times."**[19] Of these demonic whisperings is that which was stated by at-Tījānī who said:

> **"Sayyid ul-Wujūd**[20] **informed me that I am the Qutb ul-Maktūm from him and that unto me is the ability to speak with him while awake and not [merely] in dreams."**

---

[19] Mentioned by Ibn ul-'Imād in *Shadharāt udh-Dhahab*, vol.8, p.54 yet there has been much confusion and muddling in this volume of the book due to the inventions [and tampering] of the Sūfīs that are found within it, may Allāh forgive us and him.

[20] [TN] i.e. Prophet Muhammad ﷺ.

Then he said:

> He informed, while awake, and not [merely] in a
> dream, that I am from the truthful ones and he said to
> me: "All who see you are from the truthful, all who are
> good to you are from the truthful, all who give you food
> to eat will enter Paradise with neither accounting nor
> obstacles."[21]

Muhammad Aslam mentioned that the senior Tablīghīs of India
say:

> The Deoband Madrasah was established by the Prophet
> ﷺ and he would sometimes come to this abode (i.e.
> Deoband) with his companions and Khulafā' in order
> to exact the account of the Madrasah.

It is mentioned that one of their seniors sat with as-Siddīq, 'Umar,
and 'Uthmān ﷺ on a number of occasions. And that he met al-
Bukhārī, while awake and not during sleep (!), and gained an *ijāzah*
in Sahīh ul-Bukhārī from him!? This senior also (allegedly) met al-
Badr al-'Aynī and al-Hāfidh Ibn Hajar and gained an *ijāzah* from

---

[21] Muhammad bin Safiuddīn al-Hanafi, *as-Sa'āqat ul-Muhriqah 'ala'l-Mutasawwifah*,
pp.41-42 and Abū Bakr al-Jazā'irī, *Ila't-Tasawwuf Yā 'Ibādallāh!*, pp.59-60.

them both in their explanations of Sahīh ul-Bukhārī!?[22] Al-'Īdrūsī
mentioned in *an-Nūr us-Sāfir*, p.151:

---

[22] Shaykh Taqiuddīn al-Hilālī, *as-Sirāj ul-Munīr fī Tanbīh Jama'āt it-Tablīgh 'ala Akhtā'ihim* [The Gleaming Torch in Bringing to Attention of the Tablighi Jama'āt their Errors], pp.16-18; SayfurRahmān Ahmad, *Nadhrah 'Ābirah I'tibāriyyah Hawla'l-Jama'āt at-Tablīghiyyah*, p.27; *al-Qawl al-Balīgh fī't-Tahdhīr min Jama'āt it-Tablīgh* [The Profound Statement in Warning Against the Tablighi Jama'āt], p.7, 10-13, 27, 57, 63, 71, 81-82, 108, 132, 141, 217.

Also refer to their own books such as: *Malfūdhāt Muhammad Ilyās*, p.45; Abu'l-Hasan an-Nadwī, *Maulānā Muhammad Ilyās wa Da'watuhu ad-Dīniyyah* [Maulana Muhammad Ilyās and his Religious Preaching], p.84; *Sīrat Muhammad Yūsuf* [The Biography of Muhammad Ilyās], p.99; *Majālis udh-Dhikr*, pp.11-12 and *Irshādāt wa Maktūbāt Shaykh Muhammad Ilyās*, [Ordinances and Writings of Shaykh Muhammad Ilyās], p.35.

For more on the misguidance of Jama'āt ut-Tablīgh in their dependence on dreams refer to an-Najmī, *al-Mawrad al-'Adhab az-Zilāl fīmā Intaqada 'ala Ba'dh il-Manāhij ad-Da'wiyyah min al-'Aqā'id wa'l-'A'māl* ; Sayyid Tālib ur-Rahmān, *Kashf us-Sitār 'ammā Tahamalahu Ba'dh ad-Da'wāt min Akhtār* [Removing the Covers from the Dangers that Some Forms of Preaching Hold], pp.89-90; *Jama'āt ut-Tablīgh fī Shabhih al-Qārat il-Hindiyyah* [The Tablighi Jama'āt in the Indian Sub-Continent], p.22 – this book is particularly important as the author transmits from their source reference books which support what was transmitted before.

"Some of the Sūfī Awliyā were honoured to have visited the Prophetic grave and they composed poetry in praise of the Prophet ﷺ which mentioned:

So if it is said "if you truly visited why did you come back?' O Master of the Messengers, what should we say?

"Say to them: 'we returned with all virtue and gained the Furū' and the Usūl'(!)"

This miskīn also mentioned on page 276 in the biography of Abū Diyā' 'AbdurRahmān bin 'AbdulKarīm al-Ghaythī:

He saw the Prophet ﷺ with his very own eyes[23] present in one of his gatherings, and at this he felt *khushū'* (humility), *khudū'* (devotion), *sakīnah* (tranquility) and *rahma* (mercy) – the likes of which were not seen in other gatherings.

In affirming this belief they have a number of stories which the reader will find strange along with their odd method of deduction. By Allāh this is due to their shameful misguidance, their strange blend, their craziness and their aversion from the *madhhab* of the *Salaf* which the Companions of the Prophet ﷺ and those after them from Ahl ul-'Ilm were upon. What is truly strange is that as-

---

[23] **[TN]** the Arabic word here actually states "eyeballs" so as to emphasis it!

Suyūṭī holds that such wake-time visions are true and he even supports the belief in a separate book on the matter entitled *Tanwīr ul-Halak fī Ruʾyat in-Nabī waʾl-Malak* [Enlightening the Destroyed Regarding Visions of the Prophet and the Angels] which is extant within *al-Hāwī liʾl-Fatāwā*, vol.2, p.255. In the book he brings some *fatāwā* and *ahādīth* which are not even connected to the issue and then he fills the book with accounts of dreams and rejected superstitious stories which are only promoted by weak-minded idiotic people! Of this is when he states on page 39 (Dār ul-Amīn Print):

> **Shaykh Khalīfah bin Mūsā had many visions of Allāh's Messenger ﷺ while awake and not in dreams... he saw him 17 times on one particular night and on one of those nights the Prophet ﷺ said to him: "O Khalīfah do not be annoyed with me, many Awliyā have died out of grief of seeing me."**

This story and the likes of it are mere claptrap promoted by those who are poor in knowledge and reflection. Yet when we contemplate on this[24], this contains a censure and an insult to our Prophet ﷺ, because how can the servant [of Allāh] die due to grief of seeing the Prophet ﷺ in reoccurring visions?! This is, by Allāh, a

---

[24] If it is intended dying out of grief of not seeing the Prophet ﷺ then this would be understandable, but if this is not intended then a refutation is shortly to follow.

defamation and an insult because the most noble Awliyā' of this Ummah saw our Prophet ﷺ such as Abū Bakr, 'Umar, 'Uthmān, 'Ali and others and it only increased their hearts with life, light, brightness and acceptance of good in all its manifestations. So how can it be said after that, that some Awliyā' died out of grief of having visions of Allāh's Messenger?! What is strange is that as-Suyūṭī affirms this belief in many of his works such as *Nudhm ul-'Aqyān*, p.163; *Maqāmah*, vol.2, p.945 (his *Sharh*); *ad-Dībāj 'ala Sahīh Muslim bin al-Hajjāj*, vol.5, pp.284-285 and other works.[25] He transmitted the possibility of the aforementioned wake-time vision from a group of Ahl ul-'Ilm such as: Ibn al-'Arabī, Ibn Abī Jamrah, al-Ghazālī, 'Izzaddīn bin 'AbdusSalām and others.[26] Yet

---

[25] Ascribed to him by Muhammad Salīm Hamāmī in his commentary on *Daw' ush-Shams* by as-Sayādī, in vol.1, p.175 he states that some of the Awliyā' such as Ahmad ar-Rifā'ī were blessed by Allāh to meet and kiss the hand of the Prophet ﷺ. Yet upon inspection it is evident that the book is not by him as I explained in my book *Qasas la Tuthbat* [Unsubstantiated Stories], vol.3, pp.191-192.

[26] Many have authored works on this topic, such as:

❖ Yūsuf al-Khlūtī, *Tanbīh al-Ghaybī fī Ru'yat in-Nabī ﷺ* – a work mentioned by the author of *Kashf udh-Dhunūn*, vol.1, p.488.

❖ Al-Amāsī – which az-Ziriklī indicated was a work by al-Amāsī that he published.

❖ Al-Hanbalī Zādah, *Hūr ul-Khiyām wa 'Adhrā' Dhuwi'l-Hiyām fī Ru'yat Khayr il-Anām fī'l-Yaqadhah kamā fī'l-Manām* – mentioned by the author of *Kashf udh-Dhunūn*, vol.1, p.694 and in *Hidāyat ul-'Ārifīn*, vol.2, p.248

despite this school of thought being devoid of clear authentic evidences, it is still firmly believed in by the Ṣūfīs who base many rulings on them, rulings related to their *deen* and *dunyā*. As-Suyūtī, may Allāh forgive him and us, supports their (Ṣūfī) madhhab with separate independent works on the topic! He says in *Tanwīr ul-Halak*,[27] pp.48-49:

It has been relayed from some Awliyā' that he ﷺ attended some of the *fiqh* gatherings of the Fuqahā' and in one incident a faqīh relayed a hadīth and a walī of Allāh said to the faqīh: "this hadīth is bātil." The faqīh said to the Walī:

❖ Al-Bustāmī, *Durrat un-Nuqād fī Ru'yat in-Nabī ﷺ fī Khiyāl ir-Ruqād* – a work mentioned by the author of *Kashf udh-Dhunūn*, vol.1, p.744

❖ Shamsuddīn al-Hanafī has a manuscript which is preserved in Dār ul-Kutub al-Misriyyah entitled *Tablīgh ul-Marām fī Bayān Haqīqat Ru'yatihi ﷺ fī'l-Yaqadhah wa'l-Manām*

❖ 'AbdulQādir bin Husayn Maghzīl, *al-Kawākib uz-Zāhirah fī Ijtimā' al-Awliyā' Yaqadhatan bi Sayyid id-Dunyā' wa'l-Ākhir* [The Gleaming Stars in the Gathering of the Awliyā' with the Master of the Worldly Life and Hereafter] – there is a copy of this in the *Azhariyyah Library*.

[27] Refer to my book *Qasas la Tuthbat* [Unsubstantiated Stories], vol.3, pp.197 and as-Sakhāwī authored a refutation of as-Suyūtī entitled *Irshād wa'l-Maw'idhah li Zā'im Ru'yat an-Nabī ﷺ ba'da Mawtihi fī'l-Yaqadhah* . I tried to find a manuscript copy of this yet I could not find it even though I looked very hard for it, refer to my book *Mu'allifāt as-Sakhāwī*, pp.49-50.

"Where did you get this from?" The Walī said: "From the Prophet ﷺ who is floating above your head saying 'I did not say this hadīth'. Then it was unveiled for the faqīh to see Allāh's Messenger ﷺ."

By Allāh contemplate on this understanding of the *deen* wherein the statement of a Faqeeh based on the proofs of Allāh's Book and the Sunnah of His Messenger is rejected in favour of accepting *Kashf* and *Khayāl* (imagined circumstances)! An example of this confusion is what was relayed by 'AbdulGhanī an-Nāblusī in his travels entitled *al-Haqīqah wa'l-Majāz*, vol. 'Q', p.428, also transmitted from him by an-Nabhānī in *Jawāhir ul-Bihār*, vol.3, pp.1363-1364 from as-Sayyid ash-Sharīf Ahmad bin 'Abdul'Azīz al-Maghribī:

> He used to meet with the Prophet ﷺ on a number of occasions and one time when he was sick he asked the Prophet if it was allowed to smoke and the Prophet ﷺ remained silent and did not answer. Then he (ﷺ) instructed him to use it (i.e. smoking).[28]

Muhammad bin 'Alawī al-Mālikī also supports this *madhhab* (that the Prophet can be seen during wake-time) in his book *adh-*

---

[28] Also refer to al-Mar'ī al-Karamī al-Hanbalī, *Tahqīq ul-Burhān fī Sha'n id-Dukhān* (my edit – i.e. Mashhūr Hasan), p.57.

Dhakhā'ir al-Muhammadiyyah, as does Hasan bin Muhammad Shaddād bin 'Umar in his vile book *Kayfiyyat ul-Wusūl li'r-Ru'yat Sayyidinā ar-Rasūl* [How to Obtain Visions of Our Master, the Messenger]. In this book he also drinks from this innovation and supports what al-'Alawī mentions. You should know dear reader that all they can use is the hadīth *"whoever sees me in a dream will see me while awake"*; yet this is not a proof at all and we mentioned before the difference in regards to the accuracy of the wording from him ﷺ. For this reason Abu'l-'Abbās al-Qurtubī ﷲ was stern on those who had this opinion and stated in *al-Mufhim*, vol.6, pp.22-23:

> Even weak-minded people comprehend the corruption of this belief! For it necessitates that none can see him except with the image that he (ﷺ) died upon; and it necessitates that two people at the same time cannot see him (ﷺ); and it necessitates that he is alive today and that he leaves his grave and walks among people, speaking to and mixing with them as he did during his first life. And it necessitates that his grave becomes vacated of his body and that when visited his noble body is not in the grave and so people convey salāms to one who is absent from the grave... these are ignorant

beliefs which are not adhered to by whoever has even a whiff of intelligence...[29]

As for their use of the hadīth *"whoever sees me in a dream will see me while awake"* is not a proof upon deliberation. The intent of the hadīth is **"...will see me on the Day of Judgement with a special vision due to being close to me"**. Or it can mean **"whoever sees me in a dream will see me while awake on the Day of Judgement but it is not a condition to be a special vision"**. For this reason, ad-Damāmīnī ﷻ[30] stated:

This is a glad-tiding for the seer that he will die upon Islām, because one will not see the Prophet on the Day of Judgement except for the person who died upon Islām.[31]

---

[29] These words of his were transmitted from him by al-Ḥāfidh in *al-Fath*, vol.14, p.412; al-Qastalānī, *al-Mawāhib al-Laduniyyah*, vol.2, p.673; al-Munāwī, *al-Fayd*, vol.6, p.173; also refer and compare with what was stated by al-'Aynī in *'Umdat ul-Qārī*, vol.16, pp.280-281.

[30] [TN] Abū 'Abdallāh Badruddīn Muhammad ibn Abī Bakr ibn 'Umar al-Qurashī al-Mahzūmī ad-Damāmīnī (d. 827AH/1424 CE). He was an eminent Egyptian scholar and grammarian born at Alexandria, he authored *Tuhfat ul-Gharīb, Sharh Mughnī al-Labīb* and other works.

[31] *Fath ul-Bārī*, vol.14, p.413; *Fayd ul-Qadīr*, vol.6, p.172; *as-Sawā'iq ul-Mursalah ash-Shihābiyyah*, pp.98-99 and compare with at-Tuwayjurī, *al-Qawl ul-Balīgh*, pp.112-113.

Ibn ul-Jawzī ﷺ stated in *Sayd ul-Khātir* (Dār ul-'Ilmiyyah Print), pp.348-349:

The issue of having visions of the Prophet ﷺ has been problematic for the people as the apparentness of the hadīth indicates that one will truly see him, and among the people are those who see him be they old, young, sick and healthy. The answer to this is:

Those who think that the body of Allāh's Messenger ﷺ which is in Madeenah comes out of the grave and attends the places where he is seen, then this is ignorance which is unrivalled! He is seen at one time by a thousand people in a thousand different places in different forms, how can this be possible for one person?! What are seen are just images of him and not him in person, so the meaning of the hadīth *"whoever sees me has definitely seen me"* is: sees my likeness which is correctly known and with which the sought-after benefit can be gained.

When Husayn ibn Ahmad, one of the Sūfī propagators of this claptrap in India claimed that the Prophet ﷺ and all of the Prophets have a real life in the graves wherein they leave their graves when they wish – Ahl ul-'Ilm refuted him. Shaykh Muhammad Taqiuddīn al-Hilālī ﷺ stated:

Husayn Ahmad's saying "because the Prophets are alive with a real life which is not that of the Barzakh" – is a lie and falsehood! No one said this before him because life is of two types and there is not a third type that they have except for the life of the people of Paradise. The worldly life is opposite to death and the life of the barzakh combines between the death of the body and the life of the soul; as for the people of Paradise then it is more virtuous than the two aforementioned types as there is no death, sickness or grief within it. Yet this Dajjāl (i.e. Husayn bin Ahmad) added a fourth possibility of life which only exists in his imagination. Husayn bin Ahmad was also the one who gave a fatwa saying that it is not permissible in the Sharī'ah for Muslims in Pakistan to be independent (from colonialism), he must have meant in the Sharī'ah of Shaytān! Thus, he wanted the Muslims in India to remain under the rule of their idolatrous enemies; this is the Sharī'ah according to him, to act in submission to the idolaters and to defame the Muslims. Does he disbelieve in when Allāh says:

﴿ إِنَّكَ مَيِّتٌ وَإِنَّهُم مَّيِّتُونَ ﴾

"Indeed, you are to die, and indeed, they are to die."

{az-Zumar (39): 30}

﴿ وَمَا مُحَمَّدٌ إِلَّا رَسُولٌ قَدْ خَلَتْ مِن قَبْلِهِ ٱلرُّسُلُ أَفَإِيْن مَّاتَ أَوْ قُتِلَ ٱنقَلَبْتُمْ عَلَىٰ أَعْقَـٰبِكُمْ وَمَن يَنقَلِبْ عَلَىٰ عَقِبَيْهِ فَلَن يَضُرَّ ٱللَّهَ شَيْئًا وَسَيَجْزِى ٱللَّهُ ٱلشَّـٰكِرِينَ ﴾

"Muhammad is not but a messenger. [Other] messengers have passed on before him. So if he was to die or be killed, would you turn back on your heels [to unbelief]?" *{Āli 'Imrān (3): 144}*

And does he deny what Abū Bakr as-Siddīq stated when he said: "Whoever worships Muhammad, then Muhammad has died; but whoever worships Allāh then Allāh is Ever-Living and does not die"? Or does he deny the other verses as he usually does due to his confusion and craziness?![32]

Al-'Allāmah Hamūd at-Tuwayjurī ﴾ stated in his book *al-Qawl ul-Balīgh*, p.81:

The statement of Husayn Ahmad that "the Prophets are alive with a real life which is not the Barzakh" necessitates a number of void and invalid views, such as:

---

[32] *As-Sirāj ul-Munīr*, pp.26-27

That the Prophets walk on earth like those alive do, and that they eat, drink and need to use the toilet like those alive do and that they are apparent among people so that people see them, sit with them and mix with them. All of these aspects are *bāṭil* and every intelligent person knows that this is falsehood. To say such a thing is folly and madness, for such things do not emanate from one who even has the slightest morsel of intelligence! It only emanates from one who is mentally deranged!

Of the falsities that this view of Husayn Ahmad necessitates is that: it would mean that the grave of the Prophet ﷺ becomes vacant as his noble body is not there and the same for all of the Prophets. Every intelligent person knows that this is falsehood! Only one who has a problem with his mind would say such a thing!

Of the falsities that this view of Husayn Ahmad necessitates is that: it includes denial of the texts which clearly indicate that the Prophet ﷺ died and that all of creation die, such as where Allāh says,

$$﴿ إِنَّكَ مَيِّتٌ وَإِنَّهُم مَّيِّتُونَ ﴾$$

"Indeed, you are to die, and indeed, they are to die."
{az-Zumar (39): 30}

39

﴿ وَمَا مُحَمَّدٌ إِلَّا رَسُولٌ قَدْ خَلَتْ مِن قَبْلِهِ ٱلرُّسُلُ أَفَإِيْن مَّاتَ أَوْ قُتِلَ ٱنقَلَبْتُمْ عَلَىٰ أَعْقَـٰبِكُمْ وَمَن يَنقَلِبْ عَلَىٰ عَقِبَيْهِ فَلَن يَضُرَّ ٱللَّهَ شَيْئًا وَسَيَجْزِى ٱللَّهُ ٱلشَّـٰكِرِينَ ﴾

"Muhammad is not but a messenger. [Other] messengers have passed on before him. So if he was to

unbelief]?" *{Āli ʾImrān (3): 144}*

﴿ كُلُّ نَفْسٍ ذَآئِقَةُ ٱلْمَوْتِ وَإِنَّمَا تُوَفَّوْنَ أُجُورَكُمْ يَوْمَ ٱلْقِيَـٰمَةِ ﴾

"Every soul will taste death, and you will only be given your [full] compensation on the Day of Resurrection." *{Āli ʾImrān (3): 185}*

﴿ وَمَا جَعَلْنَا لِبَشَرٍ مِّن قَبْلِكَ ٱلْخُلْدَ أَفَإِيْن مِّتَّ فَهُمُ ٱلْخَـٰلِدُونَ . كُلُّ نَفْسٍ ذَآئِقَةُ ٱلْمَوْتِ وَنَبْلُوكُم بِٱلشَّرِّ وَٱلْخَيْرِ فِتْنَةً وَإِلَيْنَا تُرْجَعُونَ ﴾

"And We did not grant to any man before you eternity [on earth]; so if you die — would they be eternal? Every soul will taste death. And We test you with evil and with good as trial; and to Us you will be returned." *{al-Anbiyā' (21): 34-35}*

﴿ كُلُّ مَنْ عَلَيْهَا فَانٍ . وَيَبْقَىٰ وَجْهُ رَبِّكَ ذُو ٱلْجَلَـٰلِ وَٱلْإِكْرَامِ ﴾

"Everyone upon the earth will perish, And there will remain the Face of your Lord, Owner of Majesty and Honour." *{ar-Raḥmān (55): 26-27}*

So if Husayn Ahmad, and others from the Jam'āt ut-Tablīgh Shaykhs, view that the Prophets are alive with a real life and that their Jama'āh and seniors have the fortune of attending gatherings with the Prophet ﷺ while awake and not in dreams, and they view the invalidity of what was believed in by Shaykh ul-Islām Muhammad bin 'AbdulWahhāb and his followers that the lives of the Prophets was for that which they did in the world and after that they and their followers will die – what is their answer to those texts which indicate that death is general for all of the Prophets and other humans? What is their answer to the many *aḥādīth* which mention the death and burial of the Prophet ﷺ? For it is confirmed from him that he said

ﷺ: *"I will be the first to come out of the earth on the day of Judgement"*[33], so what is their answer to this?

If they have no sound answer to these verses which have been mentioned and to the *ahādīth* which indicate the death of the Prophet ﷺ and that he is in the grave until the Day of Judgement – it is obligatory on them to return to the truth which indicate this in the Book, Sunnah and what the *Salaf us-Sālih* understood from the Sahābah and those who followed them in goodness. This is: the belief of the death of the Prophet and other humans, and the belief that the Prophets and others who have passed are dead and still in their graves where they will remain up until the Day of Judgement; and that the first who will come out of the ground (i.e. grave) on the Day of Judgement will be Allāh's Messenger ﷺ – and all of this is the correct belief. Whatever opposes this is corrupt and Shaytān has beautified this to his Sūfī and Tablīghī allies.

Allāh says:

---

[33] Al-Bukhārī, hadīth no.2411; Muslim, hadīth no.2374; Imām Ahmad, *Musnad*, vol.3, hadīth no.3302 – and from others from the hadīth of Abū Sa'īd al-Khudrī ؓ and also from Ibn 'Abbās, Abū Hurayrah, Anas, 'Ubādah bin as-Sāmit, Ibn 'Umar, 'Abdullāh bin Salām, Wāthilah bin al-Asqa' and others with similar wordings.

﴿ وَمَن يَكُنِ ٱلشَّيْطَنُ لَهُۥ قَرِينًا فَسَآءَ قَرِينًا ﴾

"And he to whom Satan is a companion – then evil is he as a companion." *{an-Nisā' (4): 38}*

﴿ وَمَن يَعْشُ عَن ذِكْرِ ٱلرَّحْمَنِ نُقَيِّضْ لَهُۥ شَيْطَنًا فَهُوَ لَهُۥ قَرِينٌ

· وَإِنَّهُمْ لَيَصُدُّونَهُمْ عَنِ ٱلسَّبِيلِ وَيَحْسَبُونَ أَنَّهُم مُّهْتَدُونَ ﴾

"And whoever is blinded from remembrance of the Most Merciful – We appoint for him a devil, and he is to him a companion. And indeed, the devils avert them from the way [of guidance] while they think that they are [rightly] guided." *{az-Zukhruf (43): 36-37}*

﴿ فَرِيقًا هَدَىٰ وَفَرِيقًا حَقَّ عَلَيْهِمُ ٱلضَّلَلَةُ ۗ إِنَّهُمُ ٱتَّخَذُواْ

ٱلشَّيَطِينَ أَوْلِيَآءَ مِن دُونِ ٱللَّهِ وَيَحْسَبُونَ أَنَّهُم مُّهْتَدُونَ ﴾

"A group [of you] He guided, and a group deserved [to be in] error. Indeed, they had taken the devils as allies instead of Allāh while they thought that they were guided." *{al-A'rāf (7): 30}*

These verses are to be applied to the Tablīghīs who claim that the Prophets are alive in a *real and actual sense* and that

43

their Jama'āh and seniors have the fortune of having gatherings with the Prophet ﷺ while awake and not in dreams.

Within these answers and others, the correct meaning of the hadīth is apparent along with its intent. Thus, the innovation has no proof for it! This is also what al-'Allāmah al-Alūsī ﷲ supports in *Rūh ul-Ma'ānī* (Dār ul-'Ilmiyyah Print), vol.5, pp.209-210, as did al-Qastalānī before him in *Mawāhib ul-Laduniyyah,* vol.2, p.666 – who transmitted from al-Ghazālī, at-Taybī, his Shaykh Ibn Hajar and others. So we can gather from the answer about his saying *"...he will see me while awake..."* the following points:

1. As a likeness or similarity, as indicated by him saying *"...as if he sees me while awake..."*
2. That it means: *"...he will see me while awake"* in a real way or via interpretation.
3. That it is specific to the people of his time who believed in him before seeing him.
4. That he will be seen in a mirror if this is possible. Al-Hāfidh Ibn Hajar stated: "This is of the most unlikely possibilities."[34]

---

[34] This is reported from Ibn 'Abbās ﵁ that he saw Allāh's Messenger ﷺ in a dream and then produced a mirror from the home of one of the wives of the believers and saw Allāh's Messenger ﷺ in it. Al-Hāfidh responded to this in *al-Fath,* vol.14, p.413 and

5. That he will be seen on the Day of Judgement with an extra particularity...

6. That the intent of seeing his image is: his *deen* and his *Sharī'ah* which is interpreted based on what the seer sees in terms of addition, deficiency, bad or evil.[35]

We say: what is most apparent in light of the Sharī'ah in refuting the Sūfī explanation of the hadīth is that: such an explanation has not been confirmed from any of the noble Companions ﷺ who have the most *īmān* out of this Ummah, have the most *yaqīn* in the Ummah and possess the most knowledge and understanding. In the same way they had the most love and veneration of Allāh's Messenger ﷺ to the extent that Anas bin Mālik ﷺ used to see Allāh's Messenger ﷺ in a vision every night. Anas ﷺ used to say: "There is not a night except that I see within in it (i.e. in a vision) my close friend (ﷺ)" and then he would burst into tears. Al-Muthanā bin Sa'īd ad-Dubbī ﷺ stated:

Ibn Abī Jamrah also transmitted this as did al-Qastalānī *in al-Mawāhib*, vol.2, pp.666-667 and al-Haytamī in *Ashraf ul-Wasā'il*, pp.596-597.

[35] This is transmitted from al-Hāfidh in *al-Fath*, vol.14, pp.413-414 and it is also with al-Qastalānī in *al-Mawāhib ul-Laduniyyah*, vol.2, p.666 and ash-Shiblī, *Ākām ul-Marjān*, pp.182-183.

I heard Anas ؓ say: 'There are few nights which pass by except that I see within them my beloved one, Allāh's Messenger ﷺ and when Anas would say this tears would come to his eyes.'[36]

With all this, it is not confirmed that he saw Allāh's Messenger ﷺ in a real sense (i.e. during wake-time) after his death or that he met him and spoke to him or that the Prophet ﷺ instructed Anas or the Ummah with specific things as has happened with some of the Sūfī Dajājilah [excessive liars] and those who follow their follow.

So with the knowledge that the Companions had the distinguished honour they went through tribulations such as: the differing between as-Siddīq and Fāṭimah ؓ in the issue of inheritance; also the differing on the Day of al-Jamal and Siffīn; and what happened before during the Riddah Wars; and the issue of the compilation of the Qur'ān; and the succession of as-Siddīq before that – and other *fitan* before and after. Yet with all this it has not

---

[36] Reported by Imām Aḥmad, *Musnad*, vol.3, p.216 and Imām Aḥmad stated: "**Abū Sa'īd (the freed slave of Banī Hāshim) narrated to us: ...al-Muthanā narrated to us**" and then he mentioned the report. The *isnad* is Saḥīḥ n the conditions of al-Bukhārī *(rahimahullāh)*. It was also reported by Ibn Sa'd, *at-Tabaqāt*, vol.7, p.20; Ibn 'Asākir, *Tārīkh* (Dār ul-Fikr Print), vol.9, p.358 – via the route of Muslim bin Ibrāhīm from al-Muthanna; al-Haythamī, *al-Majma'*, vol.7, p.182 and he said: "**Its men are those of the Saḥīḥ.**"

been transmitted from any of them that they saw Allāh's Messenger ﷺ while they were awake, or in a dream, and asked him for the way out of these tribulations which affected the Ummah. This in itself is sufficient in refuting their Sūfī statements and explaining their obscurities, which in this issue are dangerous.[37] For this reason, al-Qastalānī ﷺ stated in *al-Mawāhib al-Laduniyyah*, vol.7, pp.292-293, *Sharh uz-Zurqānī*:

> As for seeing him ﷺ while awake after his death ﷺ then our Shaykh said: "This possibility of this has not reached us from any of the Sahābah or from those after them (from the Tābi'īn and Atbā' Tābi'īn)." Fātimah grieved over the loss of the Prophet ﷺ and she died six months after he died, according to the most authentic account. Her house was next to his noble grave yet it was not transmitted from her that she saw the Prophet ﷺ during the period that she was not with him.

Al-Qastalānī also states in vol.7, pp.300-301:

> So to conclude: the saying that he ﷺ can be seen after his death with the eyes while awake is something which the minds comprehend as being corrupt. Because it necessitates

---

[37] Compare with al-Maqdisī, *Masā'ib ul-Insān*, p.171l ash-Shiblī, *Ākām ul-Marjān*, p.183; al-Ālūsī, *Rūh ul-Ma'ānī* (Dār ul-'Ilmiyyah), vol.5, p.209

that he leaves his grave and walks within markets and speaks to people and people to him. Al-Qādī Abū Bakr bin al-'Arabī stated: "some of the righteous ones claimed that it can occur with the eyes." It was stated in *al-Fath*, vol.14, p.413, after mentioning the words of Ibn Abī Jamrah: "This has been a very problematic issue and if it is taken apparently then they would be Sahābah and companionship of him ﷺ would remain up until the Day of Judgement."

How nice is what the poet said:

Whoever claims that in this worldly abode,

Mustafā can be seen has certainly spoken a lie[38]

Al-'Allāmah 'Abdul'Azīz bin Bāz ﷲ stated:

The truth about which there is no doubt is that the Messenger ﷺ cannot be seen while one is awake after his death ﷺ. Whoever from the Sūfi persuasion claims that he has seen the Prophet ﷺ while awake or that the Prophet ﷺ has attended a Mawlid celebration and the likes has seriously erred in a vile way, has been deceived to the utmost, has fallen into a serious error and has opposed the

---

[38] *Al-Mawāhib al-Laduniyyah*, vol.2, p.674 and he ascribed it to the Shaykh of Imām Muslim, also refer to *al-Mawāhib bi'sh-Sharh uz-Zurqānī*, vol.7, p.301.

Book, Sunnah and the *ijmā'* of Ahl ul-'Ilm. Because the dead will only come out of their graves on the Day of Judgement and not in the worldly life as Allāh says:

﴿ ثُمَّ إِنَّكُم بَعْدَ ذَٰلِكَ لَمَيِّتُونَ . ثُمَّ إِنَّكُمْ يَوْمَ ٱلْقِيَـٰمَةِ تُبْعَثُونَ ﴾

"Then indeed, after that you are to die. Then indeed you, on the Day of Resurrection, will be resurrected." *{al-Muminūn (23): 15-16}*

Allāh informed that the resurrection of the dead will be on the Day of Judgement and not in the worldly life and whoever says opposite to that is a liar who has made a clear lie or he is mistaken who has been deceived as he does not know the truth which was known by the *Salaf us-Sālih* which the companions of Allāh's Messenger ﷺ and those who followed them with goodness were upon.[39]

The intent therefore after this presentation is that the belief of the possibility of seeing Allāh's Messenger ﷺ while awake and not [just] in dreams is a *bātil* belief according to the people of knowledge. The Mutasawwifah [Sūfis] past and present have adhered to this belief and have built palaces upon this with adorned and corrupted

---

[39] Imām Bin Bāz, *at-Tahdhīr min al-Bida'*, p.18.

speech. They are the most famous for adhering to this belief especially the Tijānī sect and they mainly utilise as a proof for this belief the hadīth of Abū Hurayrah ؓ: *"Whoever sees me in a dream will see me while awake"* – and this is not a proof as has preceded. Dr 'Ali bin Muhammad discussed their belief within his book *at-Tijāniyyah* (al-'Āsimah Print), pp.122-128:

> **Firstly:** The hadīth of this narration is not a clear text about seeing the Prophet ﷺ while awake after his death in the worldly life as the Tijānīs claim, rather the hadīth contains some possibilities and for this reason the 'Ulama differed as to its meaning and interpreted it with a variety of interpretations:

> Ibn ut-Tīn stated: "The intended meaning of the hadīth is: whoever believes in him during his lifetime but did not actually see him, as he is absent from him; this is a glad-tiding to all who believe in him yet did not see him, and that it is a must to see him while awake before he dies."

> Ibn Battāl said: "It means: one will see the interpretation of the vision when awake and its true manifestation."[40]

---

[40] He stated this interpretation is in *Sharh ul-Bukhārī*, vol.9, p.527: **"It means: the affirmation of the vision when awake and its true manifestation."**

It has been also said that it means: resemblance, because in the second narration it says *"...it will be as if he has seen me while awake."* It was also said that the hadīth means: "...or will see him in the Hereafter as this is a glad-tiding to the one who sees him that he will die as a Muslim because no one sees a vision indicating such special closeness except one who will die upon Islām – this is the view of ad-Damāmīnī and was also supported by Muhammad al-Khadr ash-Shinqītī, and this is the view that I incline towards."

It has also been said that it means: he ﷺ will be seen in a mirror if that is possible, and this is the view of Ibn Abī Jamrah. Al-Hāfidh Ibn Hajar stated: "This is of the unlikeliest possibilities."

It has also been said: that he ﷺ will be really seen in the worldly life and speak to the seer.

Secondly: This last possibility is *bātil* from two aspects:

First: it is impossible according to the Divine Legislation; the Prophet ﷺ died and completed his life so he cannot come back after his death before the Day of Judgement – this is impossible according to the Divine Legislation due to the belief opposing what Allāh has said:

$$\{ \text{إِنَّكَ مَيِّتٌ وَإِنَّهُم مَّيِّتُونَ} \}$$

"Indeed, you are to die, and indeed, they are to die."
{az-Zumar (39): 30}

This does not conflict with the fact that the Prophets are alive in their graves as are the *Shuhadā'* [the martyrs] – this is the life of the Barzakh which differs from this worldly life. Otherwise this would necessitate that they would be responsible (to act according to the Divine Legislation) and that they go out and fight against the enemies of Allāh – such a necessity is *bātil* and if the necessity *(lāzim)* is void what is necessitated *(al-malzūm)* is also void!

To claim that the Prophet ﷺ can be seen while awake in the worldly life after his death requires Allāh's Messenger ﷺ lying and this is impossible as he is infallible ﷺ from lying for he ﷺ said: *"Whoever sees me in a dream will see me while awake."* So the answer to the condition is that: it is well-known that many of the *Salaf* of this Ummah and those after them saw the Prophet in dreams and it is not mentioned from any of them that they saw him while awake, the report of the truthful one ﷺ do not differ.

Second: It is intellectually impossible; al-Qurtubī stated:

52

Even weak-minded people comprehend the corruption of this belief! For it necessitates that none can see him except with the image that he ﷺ died upon; and it necessitates that two people at the same time cannot see him ﷺ; and it necessitates that he is alive today and that he leaves his grave and walks among people, speaking to and mixing with them as he did during his first life. And it necessitates that his grave becomes vacated of his body and that when visited his noble body is not in the grave and so people convey salāms to one who is absent from the grave... these are ignorant beliefs which are not adhered to by whoever has even a whiff of intelligence...

What those who objected to this say is that it is possible that the Prophet ﷺ can be seen by two people in two different places at the same time just as the sun and the moon can be seen in different places at the same time by many people.[41]

The answer to this objection is that the Prophet ﷺ is a human who used to eat food and walk in the markets and

---

[41] Refer to Ibn Hajar al-Haytamī, *al-Fatāwā al-Hadīthiyyah*, pp.290, 297, 298; *Ru'yat un-Nabī ﷺ Haqq ila Qiyām is-Sa'āt*, p.29.

he did not have the form of the sun and its rising so that all people at one time could see him. Furthermore, if the Prophet ﷺ was in his house, none would see him except those with him and not those outside of his house. Likewise, the sun, if it is seen from one house, it is impossible to see its course from another house.

Thirdly: Even if we suppose that this is a correct possibility, it would not be appropriate for a scholar to make others go crazy by averting this proof back to a mere possibility. Because from the principles of *Usūl* is: **If a proof has numerous possibilities, then using these to deduce a proof is void.** So then how about a possibility which itself is nullified by its own hadīth and is rejected by the Divine Legislation and the intellect?!

Fourthly: What was transmitted from Ibn Abī Jamrah that: "whoever claims that he has a specific (vision) without anything from one making this specification (i.e. the Prophet ﷺ) is a transgressor."

This would be a rejected claim (as Ibn Abī Jamrah stated) because the hadīth is not clear and explicit in affirming that the Prophet ﷺ can be seen after his death when one is awake in this life or in the next life, so to specify it to this life is also transgression. However, the interpretation that seeing the Prophet ﷺ awake after his death in this life - is against the Divine Legislation, intellect and most of the 'Ulama hold that seeing the Prophet ﷺ while awake is only in the Hereafter and Allāh knows best.

Then Dr 'Ali bin Muhammad stated (pp.134-135):

The evidences for the impossibility of seeing the Prophet ﷺ after his death, while awake, are many and we indicated many of them within the discussion, we will summarise them as follows:

One: Seeing the Prophet ﷺ while awake is an issue of belief and beliefs are based on *tawqīf* (restriction) and nothing can be negated or affirmed except with an authentic proof that can be relied on and which the Book and the Sunnah has not relayed an affirmation of; nor did anyone claim such a belief from the Sahābah, the Tābi'īn or those who followed them. This is from the proofs of *istidlāl* (deduction) according to Ahl ul-Usūl and is known as "*Intifā' ul-Madrak*". As for the hadīth: "*...he will see me while awake...*" then we explained what the 'Ulama said about this narration and the truth in it, so refer back to what was mentioned and may Allāh grant you success to what is correct.

Two: Many dangerous events occurred within Islamic history wherein there would have been a necessity (if it was possible) of the appearance of the Prophet ﷺ. Yet with this it has not been mentioned that he ﷺ was seen by anybody while they were awake. So how could it happen for those who are inferior *(mafdūl)* and not for those who were superior *(fādil)*?! So whoever says that the Prophet ﷺ was seen while awake after his death in the worldly life has made a statement that even the weak-minded comprehend as being corrupt! Al-Qastalānī stated in *al-Mawāhib ul-Laduniyyah*: "In conclusion: the statement that seeing the Prophet ﷺ after his death with the eyes while wake is a belief that even weak-minded people comprehend as being corrupt! Because it necessitates that he leaves his grave and walks around in markets speaking to people and them to him." The statement of al-Qurtubī has been mentioned prior.[42]

Al-'Allāmah Hamūd bin 'Abdullāh at-Tuwayjurī also discussed this issue, and relayed in his book *al-Qawl ul-Qawi'*, pp.227-229 the statement of Ibn 'Alawī who said:

---

[42] Also compare with this: Ibn Kathīr, *al-Bidāyah wa'n-Nihāyah*, vol.1, p.334; Abū Hayyān, *al-Bahr ul-Muhīt*, vol.6, p.147; al-Alūsī, *Rūh ul-Ma'ānī*, vol.15, p.320; ad-Dimishqiyyah, *Shubuhāt Ahl ul-Fitnah*, vol.1, pp.392-396 and Idrīs Muhammad Idrīs, *Madhāhir ul-Inhirāfāt al-'Aqdiyyah 'inda's-Sūfiyyah*, vol.2, pp.525-537.

The one who reads about the noble Mawlid will personify his noble presence, for the Prophet ﷺ came to this world of bodily forms from the world of light before the time of his noble birth.

For the Prophet ﷺ was born with the presence of a shadow which was closer than his original image. This spirituality is supported by a spiritual form and presence and means that the Prophet has the character of his Lord for he said ﷻ in a hadīth Qudsī: *"I sit with those who mention me"* and in another narration: *"I am with those who mention me."*[43] Because he took his Lord as his example and because he had the character of his Lord he ﷺ is able to be present with those who mention him in all states wherein his noble soul

---

[43] Reported by al-Bukhārī (hadīth no. 7405); Muslim (hadīth no.2675); Ahmad, *Musnad*, vol.3, p.138 – from the hadīth of Abū Hurayrah ؓ in a *marfū* form with the wording: *"Allāh says: 'I am as how my servant thinks of Me and I am with him when he mentions Me.'"* Al-Bukhārī commented on it in his Sahīh, vol.13, p.499 and mentioned it in *Khalq Af'āl ul-'Ibād*, p.87; Ibn Mājah, hadīth no.3792; Ibn Hibbān, hadīth no.812 – with the wording *"I am with My servant when he mentions Me."*

As for the first hadīth: it was reported by ad-Daylamī in *al-Firdaws*, vol.3, p.192; hadīth no.4533 – from the hadīth of Thawbān ؓ in *marfū* form: wherein Allāh said to Mūsā *"I sit with those who mention Me."* This wording is closer to the truth and was mentioned by al-Hindī in *al-Kanz*, hadīth no.1871 and only ascribed to ad-Daylamī as has preceded.

is mentioned. The one who evokes and mentions the Prophet ﷺ this will necessitate an increase in venerating the Prophet ﷺ.

Then at-Tuwayjurī ﷲ stated commenting on this:

The answer to this is:

The words of Ibn 'Alawī in this topic include heinous and atrocious calamities, the first of them being: his claim that the Prophet ﷺ is present, for Ibn 'Alawī stated: **"the Prophet ﷺ was born with the presence of a shadow which was closer than his original image"** – the answer to this is: this is what the extremist Sūfīs and their followers from the riffraff are deluded by, those who have minds which Shaytān plays with and he beautifies their evil actions to them and deludes them into believing that the "Prophetic spirit" is present with them when they perform their innovation of Mawlid. The statement of Allāh is to be applied to them:

﴿ وَمَن يَعْشُ عَن ذِكْرِ ٱلرَّحْمَٰنِ نُقَيِّضْ لَهُۥ شَيْطَٰنًا فَهُوَ لَهُۥ قَرِينٌ وَإِنَّهُمْ لَيَصُدُّونَهُمْ عَنِ ٱلسَّبِيلِ وَيَحْسَبُونَ أَنَّهُم مُّهْتَدُونَ ﴾

"And whoever is blinded from remembrance of the Most Merciful – We appoint for him a devil, and he is to him a companion. And indeed, the devils avert them from the way [of guidance] while they think that they are [rightly] guided." *{az-Zukhruf (43): 36-37}*

﴿ فَرِيقًا هَدَىٰ وَفَرِيقًا حَقَّ عَلَيْهِمُ ٱلضَّلَٰلَةُ ۗ إِنَّهُمُ ٱتَّخَذُواْ ٱلشَّيَٰطِينَ أَوْلِيَآءَ مِن دُونِ ٱللَّهِ وَيَحْسَبُونَ أَنَّهُم مُّهْتَدُونَ ﴾

"A group [of you] He guided, and a group deserved [to be in] error. Indeed, they had taken the devils as allies instead of Allāh while they thought that they were guided." *{al-A'rāf (7): 30}*

The Prophet ﷺ is exalted to the utmost from what the ignorant are deluded with about the presence of his soul when they perform their innovations which he himself ﷺ warned from and instructed to reject and informed the evil and misguidance of!

It should also to be said that: the presence of the shadow follows from the presence of the actual body and it is not possible to imagine the presence of a shadow without their being its respective essence from which the shadow emanates! Thus, the statement of Ibn 'Alawī necessitates that the Prophet ﷺ is present with his essence from which the shadow emanates when they perform their *bida'* of Mawlid. Yet Ibn 'Alawī himself (on pages 24 and 25 of his book) refutes those who think that the Prophet ﷺ with his actual noble body enters their *bida'* gatherings of Mawlid when they mention his birth and when they stand out of respect and veneration of him. Ibn 'Alawī himself refutes extensively those who think this and frees himself from this idea and says that it is a ruling on his noble body ﷺ which is only believed in by a deviant and an innovator and that it contains temerity, insolence and filth which would only emanate from a hateful person or a stubborn ignoramus.

Ibn 'Alawī himself states: "The Prophet ﷺ is exalted over this, he is more perfect and more honoured than it be said in regards to him that he leaves his grave with his body and attends such gatherings at certain times." These words from Ibn 'Alawī are very good even though he summarises it. However, he contradicts it on page 31 by saying: "the Prophet ﷺ is present when the following words are uttered: 'the Prophet ﷺ was born with the presence of the shadow which is closer than his original presence.'" I say: it is not hidden from the intelligent one that the presence of the shadow is not possible except after the presence of the body from which the shadow emanates. For if the body is not also present then the shadow would be non-existent! This is well-known by necessity by every intelligent person and whoever turns away from this then this proves compounded ignorance and a deficient mindset.

The second calamitous statement: his claim that the Prophet ﷺ is created with the 'character' of his Lord.

This is a very offensive thing to apply to Allāh, and it is also repulsive to apply to the Prophet ﷺ. As for it being an offense to Allāh then it is because it compares the Creator with creation and describes Him with their characteristics, as he (Ibn 'Alawī) has claimed that the Lord has a 'character' from which the Prophet ﷺ had his character, yet 'character' is a feature of creation and is not to be applied to others. Allāh says,

$$﴿ وَإِنَّكَ لَعَلَىٰ خُلُقٍ عَظِيمٍ ﴾$$

"And indeed, you are of a great moral character."
{al-Qalam (68): 4}

And Allāh says when informing about the people of Hūd that they said:

$$﴿ إِنْ هَـٰذَآ إِلَّا خُلُقُ ٱلْأَوَّلِينَ ﴾$$

"This is not but the custom of the former peoples..."
{ash-Shu'arā' (26): 137}

The *ahādīth* which praise having good character and censure bad character are many. Ibn ul-Athīr stated in *an-Nihāyah*, as did Ibn Mandhūr in *Lisān ul-'Arab*:

Al-Khuluq: with a dhammah on the lām or a sukūn. It relates to the deen, nature and temperament.

It is the inner reality of a person and his self, and the description of the self and the meaning which is specific to the self - which all equals the character of his outer form and its description and meanings.

If this is known it should also be known that it has not been mentioned in either the Book or verified Sunnah from the Prophet ﷺ that "character" has been applied to Allāh. Neither has this been reported from any of the Sahābah or those Tābi'īn who followed them in goodness. Based on this, the application of this to Allāh is a *bida'* and is *tashbīh* between Allāh and His creation[44] – Allāh has the Most Beautiful Names and the Most Exalted Attributes. Allāh has an Essence yet this does not resemble essences of creation; likewise, Allāh has Attributes yet these do not resemble the attributes of creation, Allāh says:

$$ \text{﴿ لَيْسَ كَمِثْلِهِۦ شَىْءٌۖ وَهُوَ ٱلسَّمِيعُ ٱلْبَصِيرُ ﴾} $$

"There is nothing like unto Him, and He is the Hearing, the Seeing." *{ash-Shūrā (42): 11}*

---

[44] [TN] Interestingly, the followers and students of Ibn 'Alawī are the quickest to call Ahl us-Sunnah "Mushabbihah" and "Mujassimah" – yet it seems that they need to sort their own 'aqīdah out first before making such serious accusations against Ahl us-Sunnah.

Nu'aym bin Hammād, the Shaykh of al-Bukhārī stated: "Whoever compares Allāh with His creation has disbelieved, and whoever denies something that Allāh described Himself with has disbelieved." This is what Nu'aym bin Hammād stated and this is the madhhab of Ahl us-Sunnah wa'l-Jama'ah and there is no difference among them in regards to this.

As for the repugnant application of this belief to the Messenger ﷺ then this view makes the Messenger a partner with Allāh in His Attributes and Actions. Because to say the Messenger is created with "the character of Allāh" is to describe the Messenger with Allāh's Attributes. This necessitates associating and equalising between Allāh and His Messenger ﷺ and that the he ﷺ has the character, sustains, gives life, gives death, controls the affairs and does all those things which are particular to the Lord. This is worse than the *shirk* committed by the people of Jāhiliyyah because the people of Jāhiliyyah used to single out the Lord with His Rubūbiyyah and used to commit *shirk* in Tawhīd ul-Ulūhiyyah.

The third calamitous statement: his statement: "Because he took his Lord as his example and because he had the character of his Lord he ﷺ is able to be present with those who mention him in all states wherein his noble soul is mentioned."

Answer: to say this is major *shirk*, because the meaning of "taking someone else as an example" (*at-Ta'sī bi'l-Ghayr*) is to take him as a guide so as to be like him. As for "having the character of His Character" then this is to describe him with His Attributes so as to be like Him. Ibn Mandhūr mentions in *Lisān ul-'Arab*: "Al-Uswa is al-Qudwā, so it is said "a'ta'sa bihi" which means to follow him so as to be like him." Al-Harawī stated: "Ta'sī bihi means: to follow someone's actions and take him as a guide".

Then at-Tuwayjurī stated (p.234):

As for the statement of Ibn 'Alawī that he ﷺ is **"present with those who mention him in all states wherein his noble soul is mentioned"**;

Answer: this is of the delusions of the ignoramuses, for the Prophet ﷺ said, in what was narrated by 'Abdullāh ibn Mas'ūd ﷜: *"Unto Allāh are angels which travel the earth and convey to me blessings invoked (on me) from my Ummah."* Reported by Ahmad, an-Nasā'ī and ad-Dārimī with an authentic chain of transmission according to the condition

of Imām Muslim.[45] Ibn Hibbān also reported it in his
Sahīh. It contains a refutation of the deluded idea that the
Prophet ﷺ is present with his noble soul with those who
mention him in all places. If the matter was as is claimed it
would mean that there would be no need of angels
travelling the earth to convey the salāms to the Prophet ﷺ!
Shaykh Sulaymān bin 'Abdullāh bin ash-Shaykh
Muhammad bin 'AbdulWahhāb ﷺ in *Sharh ut-Tawhīd*[46]
quoted from *al-Fatāwā al-Bazāziyyah*, one of the Hanafī
books, the author of it says: **"Our 'Ulama say: whoever
says "the souls of the Mashāiykh are present" has
disbelieved."** Shaykh Sulaymān says:

If he intends by the 'Ulama, the 'Ulama of the
Sharī'ah, then there is an ijmā' on the kufr of such a
belief; and if he intends the Hanafī 'Ulama in
particular then there is an agreement from them on
the kufr of such a belief.

---

[45] Reported by Imām Ahmad, *Musnad*, vol.1, p.387, 441, 452; an-Nasā'ī, *'Amal ul-
Yawm ul-Qiyāmah*, p.66; *al-Mujtabā*, vol.3, p.43; ad-Dārimī, vol.2, p.317; Ibn Hibbān,
914; 'AbdurRazzāq, *Musannaf*, hadīth no.3116; Ibn ul-Mubārak, *az-Zuhd*, hadīth
no.1028; al-Hākim, *al-Mustadrak*, vol.2, p.421; at-Tabarānī, hadīth nos. 10528,
10529, 10530; and also reported by others from the hadīth of Ibn Mas'ūd ﷺ.

[46] p.133

With this you know my brother that the Sūfis have certainly gone to excess in the issue of visions:

For they have made it a source of gaining knowledge to the extent that you can see many of the Sūfi cults *(turuq)* claim that their founding Shaykh had a vision of the Prophet ﷺ to perform a particular set of supplications, prayers or the like. Far be it that the Prophet ﷺ would have specified anyone with anything, as the *deen* is from Allāh and Allāh said,

﴿ ٱلۡيَوۡمَ أَكۡمَلۡتُ لَكُمۡ دِينَكُمۡ وَأَتۡمَمۡتُ عَلَيۡكُمۡ نِعۡمَتِى وَرَضِيتُ لَكُمُ ٱلۡإِسۡلَـٰمَ دِينًا ۚ فَمَنِ ٱضۡطُرَّ فِى مَخۡمَصَةٍ غَيۡرَ مُتَجَانِفٍ لِّإِثۡمٍ فَإِنَّ ٱللَّهَ غَفُورٌ رَّحِيمٌ ﴾

"This day I have perfected for you your religion and completed My favour upon you and have approved for you Islam as religion." *{al-Mā'idah (5): 3}*

This includes whoever accuses the Messenger ﷺ of hiding that which is not befitting for Prophethood, the Message and the trust, truthfulness and conveyance of the message that the Prophets are characterised with. The Ummah have concurred on not depending upon a Divinely Legislated *fatwā* from the Messenger ﷺ which has been given to someone during a dream. With this we know the level of misguidance that Sufism has reached, the legislation of which undermines the pillars of the religion of Muhammad.[47]

With these texts the intent finishes, and all praise is due to Allāh for granting success.

---

[47] Dr Ibrāhīm bin Muhammad al-Brīkān, "at-Tasawwuf fī Mīzān il-'Aql wa'n-Naql" [Sufism in the Scales of the Intellect and Text], in the journal *Majallat ul-Buhūth il-Islāmiyyah*, no.41, pp.196-197.

Fifth Issue

Some of the Mutasawwifah (Sūfīs), and others who are weak in knowledge, claim that having visions of the Prophet ﷺ is possible via (performing) specific prayers on the night of Jumu'ah and in a specific way wherein if one does it will see him on such a night. This is also a newly invented action of worship which is not affirmed from him ﷺ, from any of his companions ◌, from the Tābi'īn or the Imāms who came after them. There is no doubt that if this is the case, that it is unknown and not affirmed from those nobles, including our Prophet ﷺ. It is *bāṭil* and not permissible to practice or believe that it is allowed or permitted. This is neither a new nor strange saying which shows the insanity of the Sūfīs and their followers and this is not the first newly invented matter from these people, may Allāh guide them.

In the book *Mafātīh ul-Farj* (pp.48-53) are strange examples of prayers and acts of worship which supposedly lead to visions of the Prophet ﷺ in dreams. Examples of which include: reading *Sūrat ul-Kawthar* a thousand times along with prayers upon the Prophet ﷺ a

Seeing the Prophet ﷺ In Dreams and Visions

thousand times too.[48] Another example is: to bathe on the night of Jumu'ah and then pray two Rak'ats wherein,

$$﴿ قُلْ هُوَ ٱللَّهُ أَحَدٌ ﴾$$

"Say: 'Allāh is One.'"
{al-Ikhlās (112): 1}

...is recited a thousand times. Such a practice for this has been attributed to our Prophet ﷺ in false and fabricated *ahādīth*. In the book *al-Mawdū'āt al-Kubrā*, vol.2, pp.58-59 by Ibn ul-Jawzī it is relayed:

> Muhammad bin Nāsir informed us: Abū Sālih Ahmad bin 'AbdulMalik an-Naysabūrī informed us: Ismā'īl bin Mas'adah al-Hāfidh narrated to us: Abū Hāmid Ahmad bin Ibrāheem al-Faqīh narrated to us: Muhammad bin Muhammad bin 'Ali al-Ash'ath narrated to us: Shareeh bin 'AbdulKarīm at-Tamīmī and Abū Ya'qūb Yūsuf bin 'Ali narrated to us saying: Abu'l-Fadl Ja'far bin Muhammad bin Ja'far ibn Muhammad bin 'Ali bin al-Husayn narrated to us: Ya'lā bin 'Ubayd narrated to us from al-A'mash from Abū Sālih from Ibn 'Abbās: Allāh's Messenger ﷺ used to say: *"There is no believer who prays two Rak'ahs on the night of Jumu'ah who reads al-Fātihah in each Rak'ah and 'Qul*

---

[48] Ibn Muflih ﷺ mentions this practice in *Masā'ib ul-Insān*, p.175 and refutes such a method.

huwa Allāhu Ahad' twenty-five times and then makes taslīm and then says "Allāhumma Salli 'ala Muhammad an-Nabī al-Ummī" a thousand times – except that he will see me on the night...whoever sees me Allāh will forgive his sins."

This hadīth is inauthentic because it contains a group of unknown narrators. Then:

'Abdullāh bin 'Ali al-Muqrī informed us: Abū Mansūr Muhammad bin Muhammad bin 'Abdul'Azīz informed us: Abū Ahmad 'Ubaydillāh bin Muhammad bin Ahmad al-Fardī informed us: Abu't-Tayyib Muhammad bin Ahmad bin Mūsā bin Hārūn narrated to us: Abu'l-'Abbās Muhammad bin Ibrāhīm al-Bazūrī narrated to us: I heard Muhammad bin 'Ukāshah al-Kirmānī say: Mu'āwiyah bin Hammād al-Kirmānī informed us: from Ibn Shihāb who said: whoever bathes on the night of Jumu'ah and prays two Rak'ahs wherein he reads, **"Say: 'Allāh is One.'"** {al-Ikhlās (112): 1} a thousand times and then sleeps will see the Prophet ﷺ. Ibn 'Ukāshah said: "I did this for two years. I would bathe on every night of Jumu'ah and then pray two Rak'ahs and I recited, **"Say: 'Allāh is One.'"** {al-Ikhlās (112): 1} a thousand times hoping to have a vision of the Prophet ﷺ; then on a cold night I bathed and prayed two Rak'ahs and read within them, **"Say: 'Allāh is One.'"** {al-

Ikhlās (112): 1} a thousand times and then I went to bed and I had a dream; I got up a second time bathed and prayed two Rak'ahs and read within them **"Say: 'Allāh is One.'"** *{al-Ikhlās (112): 1}* a thousand times and by the time I had completed them it was nearing dawn. I leaned against the wall and the Prophet ﷺ came to me and he was wearing two outer garments *(burdān)*. He approached me and said to me: "HayyakAllāh yā Muhammad!"

Ibn 'Ukāshah then mentioned in a long story that certain aspects of belief were presented to him. Yet Muhammad bin 'Ukāshah is of the biggest liars and Abū Zur'ah said: **"he was a chronic liar."** Ad-Dāraqutnī said: **"he fabricates hadīth."** As you can see these reports are fabricated and have been made up by liars in order to ascribe falsehood to our Prophet ﷺ and this is only promoted by Ahl ul-Bida'. Woe to those who blindly follow [baseless] stories and ignorance.

The Huffādh and those who classify fabricated reports and narrations have supported what was stated by Ibn ul-Jawzī ﷺ in his refutation of such lies and the prohibition of acting in accordance with such made-up narrations, such as as-Suyūtī in his book *al-La'ali' ul-Masnū'ah*, vol.2, pp.64-65; Ibn 'Irāq in *Tanzīh ush-Sharī'ah*, vol.2, pp.97-98; ash-Shawkānī in *al-Fawā'id ul-Majmū'ah*, pp.69-70, nos.170, 171 and others. Abū 'Abdillāh bin Muflih ﷺ said in *Masā'ib ul-Insān*, pp.174-175:

This hadīth was fabricated and ascribed to: Ya'lā bin 'Ubayd from al-A'mash from Abū Sālih from Ibn 'Abbās and Muhammad bin Muhammad bin al-Ash'ath was accused (of fabricating it).[49] Its chain of transmission contains darknesses (due to the *majāhīl* who fabricated it and ascribed it to those mentioned above) and the text of it is of the most severe of transgression. It was mentioned in *Musnad ul-Firdaws* and a group of those who incline towards Sufism have been deceived by it and it has no basis.

The intent is that the *ahādīth* which have been relayed in regards to this act of worship are not affirmed from our Prophet ﷺ so to act by them is unlegislated, this is particularly the case when not one of the *Salaf* acted according to such a practice. The *Salaf* and the people of knowledge have highlighted that being preoccupied with something, remembering it often and evoking it is a way which can possibly lead to seeing it in a dream. This is based on the famous hadīth: *"A vision is of three types...of it: what concerns a man before his dream and then he sees it in his dream."*[50] For this reason, the righteous ones had many visions of the Prophet ﷺ while asleep not to mention the visions of the companions ﷺ as has preceded from Anas bin Mālik ﷺ. Also of this is what was mentioned by az-

---

[49] Refer to what was stated by Ibn 'Adiyy in *al-Kāmil*, vol.6, pp.301-305 and adh-Dhahabī in *al-Mīzān*, vol.4, pp.27-28.

[50] The *takhrīj* of this has preceded and more about it will soon follow.

Zawāwī in *Manāqib ul-Imām Mālik* from al-Muthannā bin Sa'īd al-Qasīr who said: I heard Mālik bin Anas ؄ say: **"I did not remain a night except that I saw within it Allāh's Messenger (ﷺ)."**[51] This is due to his increased closeness to knowledge and the narrations of the Sunnah and disseminating it. The likes of such reports are also mentioned by Abu't-Tayyib al-Qannūjī in *at-Tāj ul-Makallal*, p.357 in the biography of Muhammad ibn Muslih ad-Damīrī that:

He used to see Allāh's Messenger ﷺ once every week [in visions] and then he left his role as a judge hoping to have more visions in his sleep of Allāh's Messenger ﷺ. When he saw Allāh's Messenger ﷺ a second time, after he had left his role as a judge, he said to him: "O Allāh's Messenger! I left the role as a judge so as to increase my closeness to you, yet it did not occur as I had hoped for." Allāh's Messenger ﷺ said to him: "The relationship between you and me is via your role as a judge and the position is more suitable than you leaving it; because in your role as a judge you are occupied with rectifying yourself and my Ummah yet when you leave this role you focus on rectifying only yourself. When you increase your rectification [of not just yourself but also of others] you increase in your closeness to me."

---

[51] As is found in *Muqaddimat ul-Mudawannah* (Dār ul-'Ilmiyyah Print), vol.1, p.70.

They also mention in the biography of Burhānuddīn bin Muhammad, well-known as "Ibn ul-Bīkār":

When he would become very ill he would see Allāh's Messenger in dreams and then become cured, and he would strive to make sure that he went to bed in a state of Tahārah.[52]

Bikār bin Muhammad ﷺ stated:

'Abdullāh bin 'Awn[53] used to hope to see the Prophet ﷺ in dreams and did not see him except just before his death. He was very happy with this, and he left his house and went down the stairs to the Masjid and fell and injured his leg. He did not treat it until he died from the wound ﷺ.[54]

The likes of these reports are encouragement for the Sunnī to experience these noble visions.[55] What is intended [with these

---

[52] Ibn ul-'Imād, *Shadharāt udh-Dhahab*, vol.8, p.314

[53] **[TN]** 'Abdullāh ibn 'Awn ibn Artāt al-Basrī al-Faqīh ﷺ d. 151 AH/768 CE.

[54] Reported by Ibn Sa'd in *at-Tabaqāt*, vol.7, pp.268-269; Ibn 'Adiyy, *al-Kāmil*, vol.6, pp.169-170; Ibn 'Asākir, *Tārīkh Dimishq* (Dār ul-Fikr Print), vol.31, p.367; al-Mizzī, *Tahdhīb ul-Kāmil* (Dār ul-Fikr Print), vol.17, pp.147-148 and others.

[55] **Point of benefit:** reported by al-Azraqī in *Tārīkh Makkah*, vol.1, pp.342-343 from 'Uthmān bin Sāj who said: "It reached me from the Prophet ﷺ that he said: *"The first*

examples] is that intense longing for the Prophet ﷺ is the path to see him in a vision. Ibn ul-Qayyim said in *Miftāh Dār us-Sa'ādah*, vol.1, p.12:

> Love of something, seeking it and desiring it necessitate imagining it, whoever experiences something pleasant and its delightfulness is almost unable to remain patient when away from it. This is because the soul is an eager connoisseur and if it tastes something it will yearn for it. For this reason, if the servant tastes the sweetness of īmān, and this mixes with the window of his heart and this becomes his love ingrained into him – then nothing will be able to harm him at all.

Ibn ul-Qayyim also said in *Jalā' ul-Afhām* (my *tahqīq*)[56], pp.616-617, in mentioning the benefits of sending prayers upon the Prophet ﷺ:

---

things which will be raised will be the Rukun, the Qur'ān and visions of the Prophet (ﷺ) in dreams.''' This is da'īf due to the weakness of 'Uthmān bin Sāj who was deemed as weak by al-Hāfidh in *at-Taqrīb* and due to his weakness he mentioned the words **"It has reached me..."** as you see, refer to the words of our Shaykh, al-Albānī ﷺ, in *ad-Da'īfah*, vol.6, p.412, hadīth no.2878.

[56] **Translator's note:** i.e. Shaykh Mashhūr *(hafidhahullāh).*

It is a cause for permanent love of the Messenger ﷺ and increasing the love and doubling it. It is a link in the chain of *īmān* which is not completed except with it. For whenever the servant remembers that which he loves and evokes it in his heart, evoking its good aspects and his meaningful motives for loving it, his love of it doubles and he increases his longing for it and this conquers his heart. If he turns away from remembering it, and from evoking its good aspects in his heart, then his love of it diminishes in his heart. There is nothing which delights the eye of the loving servant more than viewing his beloved, and there is nothing which delights his heart more than remembering it and evoking its good aspects. If this is strengthened in his heart and his tongue praises and eulogizes it, and he mentions its good qualities the increase of that, or its decrease, will depend on the increase of love or the decrease of it in his heart. Feelings are a witness to this, to the extent that some poets said,

عجبت لمن يقول ذكرت حبي ... وهل أنسى فأذكر من نسيت

I was amazed at the one who says "I remembered my love",

Yet do I forget and then remember one who I have forgotten?!

This lover was amazed at the one who said "I remembered my beloved" because remembrance comes after forgetfulness. Yet if the love was perfected and complete one would not forget his beloved. (As was said):

أريد لأنسى ذكرها فكأنما ... تمثّل لى ليلى بكل سبيل

I want to forget remembering her,

Yet it is as if I visualise Laylā in every way.[57]

Here he informs that due to his love of her he is unable to forget her. Another poet said:

يراد من القلب نسيانكم ... وتأبى الطباع على الناقلِ

It is wanted from the heart to forget you,

But the nature which I carry resists this

Here he says his love of them has become natural to him and whoever wants contrary to this has left his nature. The famous parable "whoever loves a thing will increase his mention of it" and in this noble context it is befitting that I mention:

---

[57] This was stated by Kuthayr as relayed in al-Jumaḥī, *Ṭabaqāt ush-Shu'arā*, p.134; Ibn Mandhūr, *Lisān ul-'Arab* (refer to the *Shi'r*), vol.5, p.366, vol.8, p.22; also relayed by Ibn ul-Qayyim in *ad-Dā'a wa'd-Dawā'*, p.286 and in *Rawdat ul-Muhibbīn*, p.182.

[TN] Abū Hamzah Kuthayr al-Khuzā'ī al-Madanī is the male lover from the classical Arabic love story Kuthayr and Azza which is similar to the love story of Laylā and Majnūn. Ibn Ishāq stated that Kuthayr was the "best of Muslim poets". Ibn Sallām al-Jumaḥī (232 AH/846 CE) authored one of the earliest *Ṭabaqāt* of the poets.

لو شق عن قلبي... فرى وجهه ذكرك والتوحيد في سطر

If my heart was cleft asunder,

Within it would be Your remembrance and tawhīd.

This is the heart of the believer: *tawhīd* of Allāh and remembrance of His Messenger is engraved within it both of which are not removed. When something is oft-remembered this necessitates the continuous loving of the thing and forgetting it is due to the disappearance of loving it or the weakness in loving it. Allāh is ever deserving of worship and the utmost love and veneration, indeed the *shirk* which Allāh does not forgive is when a person associates with Him in love and veneration wherein the person loves and venerates the creation other than Him as one should love and venerate Allāh, Allāh says:

﴿ وَمِنَ ٱلنَّاسِ مَن يَتَّخِذُ مِن دُونِ ٱللَّهِ أَندَادًا يُحِبُّونَهُمْ كَحُبِّ ٱللَّهِ ۖ وَٱلَّذِينَ ءَامَنُوٓا۟ أَشَدُّ حُبًّا لِّلَّهِ ۗ وَلَوْ يَرَى ٱلَّذِينَ ظَلَمُوٓا۟ إِذْ يَرَوْنَ ٱلْعَذَابَ أَنَّ ٱلْقُوَّةَ لِلَّهِ جَمِيعًا وَأَنَّ ٱللَّهَ شَدِيدُ ٱلْعَذَابِ ﴾

"And [yet], among the people are those who take other than Allāh as equals [to Him]. They love them as they [should] love Allāh. But those who believe are stronger in love for Allāh." {al-Baqarah (2): 165}

Allāh informed that the Mushrik loves the partner as Allāh should be loved and that the believer is much stronger in his love of Allāh than all else.

Hasan bin Muhammad Shaddād bin 'Umar Bā 'Amr also wrote a book entitled *Kayfiyyat ul-Wusūl li'r-Ru'yat ir-Rasūl* [How to Obtain Visions of the Messenger] and it is of the worst of books which attempt to acknowledge these prayers and special acts of worship for visualising the Prophet ﷺ. To the extent that he even mentions in the book over 130 prayer formulas for visualising the Prophet in dreams. In doing so, he transmits from the main Sūfis special remembrances in special ways which include various types of innovation and *shirk* practices which we have to cut off from due to them not being from Allāh's *deen* whatsoever, rather they are from the fancies of Ahl ul-Bida' and their cults which are far from the knowledge of the Book and the Sunnah.[58]

---

[58] We do not know the condition of the book by Sulaymān al-Ahdal which is entitled *Ithāf Uli's-Safā bi'l-Khisāl al-Mawjibah li'r-Ru'yat al-Mustafā* [Gifting the People of Purity with the Ways Which Necessitate Visualising Mustafā]. It was mentioned by 'Abdullāh bin Muhammad al-Habashī in *Masādir al-Fikr al-Islāmī*, p.292 and also in *Mu'jam al-Mawdū'at al-Matrūqah*, vol.2, p.1270.

Sixth Issue

Imām an-Nawawī ﷺ was asked about seeing the Prophet ﷺ in a dream: "is this particular for the righteous people or are others also included?" He replied: **"They are seen by them (i.e. the righteous) and others."**[59]

---

[59] As is found in *Fatāwā al-Imām an-Nawawī*, p.199.

Seventh Issue

The righteous had many visions of the Prophet ﷺ and it has been famed that some from this Ummah had many visions on a regular basis. To the extent that some people classified works on this topic[60]

---

[60] Of the works which have been authored in regards to this subject are:

❖ Muhammad Kanūn, *Hidāyat ul-Muhibb wa'l-Mushtāq al-Mustahām li'r-Ru'yat man buniya 'alayhi'l-Mulk wa'l-Khilāfah fī'l-Manām 'alayhi Salāt wa's-Salām* [Guiding the Eager and Devoted Lover to Visualise the One Upon Whom Had the Dominion and Caliphate Built for, in Dreams]

❖ Muhammad 'AbdurRahīm, *Qasas wa Akhbār man Ra'ā Sayyid al-Abrār ﷺ fī'l-Manām* [Stories and Reports of Those Who Saw the Master of the Righteous in Dreams]. Egypt: 1410 AH/1990 CE.

As for the works which have not been published then they are very many and it is difficult to restrict and compile them, yet these are what I came across:

❖ Abū 'Abdullāh Muhammad al-Adh'ātī (d.727 AH/1327 CE), *Tuhfat ut-Tullāb al-Mustahām fī Ru'yat an-Nabī 'alayhi's-Salāt wa's-Salām* [A Gift for Devoted Seekers for Visualising the Prophet upon him be prayers and peace]. There is a manuscript copy of this in the As'ad Effendī Library and it was mentioned in *Kashf udh-Dhunūn*, vol.1, pp.368-369 and *Hidyat ul-'Ārifīn*, vol.2, p.146

81

❖ Al-Qalqashandī, *al-Isti'lām 'ala Ru'yat an-Nabī 'alayhis-salām fi'l-Manām*. This was mentioned by Kahālah in *Mu'jam ul-Mu'aliffīn*, vol.9, p.177.

❖ 'Abdullāh al-Bustāmī, *al-I'lām fi Ru'yat in-Nabī* ﷺ as mentioned in *Hidyat ul-'Ārifīn*, vol.1, p.452 and by Kahālah, vol.6, p.130. Al-Bustāmī also has *Ghāyat ul-I'lām fi Ru'yat an-Nabī 'alayhis-salām*, they are most probably two separate books.

❖ 'Ali al-Halabī (d. 1022 AH/1613 CE), *Bughyat Dhuwi'l-Ahlām bi-Akhbār man Farak Karbahu bi Ru'yat il-Mustafā* ﷺ *fi'l-Manām* [The Hope of those of Sound Mind with Reports of Those Who Gained Salvation via Visions of Mustafa in Dreams]. There is a manuscript copy of it in Dār ul-Kutub al-Misriyyah and another in Ghūtā, it was mentioned by the author of *Kashf udh-Dhunūn*, vol.1, p.248.

❖ Al-Judhāmī, *Haqā'iq Barakāt ul-Manām fi Marā'i il-Mustafā Khayr ul-Anām* [The Realities of the Blessings of Dreams in Seeing Mustafa the Best of Creation], mentioned in *al-Ihātah*, vol.4, p.388 and in *Nafh ut-Tayyib*, vol.6, p.145.

❖ Muhammad bin Sālim al-Hafnāwī, *Durr ut-Tanwīr fimā yata'allaq bi Ru'yat il-Bashīr an-Nadhīr* [The Gleaming Pearl Regarding Visions of the Bringer of Glad-Tidings and Warner], there is a manuscript copy of it in Dār ul-Kutub al-Misriyyah.

❖ Bakhshī Khalīfah al-Kadūsī (d. 930 AH/1524 CE), *Risālat fi Ru'yat in-Nabī* ﷺ *fi'l-Manām* [Treatise Regarding Visions of the Prophet in Dreams], it was mentioned in *Kashf udh-Dhunūn*, vol.1, p.869.

and historians also noted this in reports and biographies of people

❖ Ahmad al-Halabī al-Fāsī, *Manāhil ish-Shafā fī Ruʾyat il-Mustafā* ﷺ, mentioned in *Īdāh ul-Maknūn*, vol.2, p.564 and in *at-Tuqāt ud-Durar*, p.303.

❖ 'Ali al-Mursafi, *Hidāyat ul-Mustahām il-Mushtāq liā Ruʾyat an-Nabī* ﷺ, mentioned in *Hidyat ul-ʾĀrifīn*, vol.1, p.473 and mentioned by Brockelmann, vol.8, p.254 and there is a manuscript copy of it in Rabāt, Ahqāf and Paris.

❖ Ibn Tūlūn, *Tahqīq ul-Ahlām fī Ruʾyat in-Nabī* ﷺ *fī'l-Manām*, mentioned in *al-Falak ul-Mashūn*, p.88

❖ *Tarjumān ul-Ashwāq fī Ruʾyat Sayyid ul-Khalq 'ala'l-Itlāq*, mentioned by the author of *Muʿjam Aʿlām ul-Jazāʾir*, p.323.

❖ Ahmad al-Burdānī, *Kitāb fī'l-Manāmāt an-Nabawiyyah* [Book on Prophetic Dreams], mentioned by Kahālah in *Muʿjam ul-Muʾalliffīn*, vol.2, p.77. It comprised what the Prophet ﷺ saw in dreams, this was also mentioned by Brockelmann, vol.7, p.74.

❖ As-Samhūdī, *Nasīhat ul-Labīb fī Marāʾī al-Habīb*

❖ Al-Fāsī, *Kashf ul-Ghuyūb 'an Ruʾyat Habīb il-Qulūb* [Uncovering the Absence from Visions of the Beloved of the Hearts], mentioned in *Fahrus ul-Fahāris*, p.602 and in *Shajarat un-Nūr iz-Zakiyyah*, p.333

❖ Ibn 'Arabī as-Sūfi, *al-Mubashirāt li'l-Ahlām fīmā Rawī 'an Rasūlillāh* ﷺ *min il-Akhbār fī'l-Manām* [Glad-Tidings from the Reports Regarding What Has Been Narrated from Allāh's Messenger in Dreams], mentioned in *Hidyat ul-ʾĀrifīn*, vol.2, p.120 and also see *Muʾallifāt Ibn 'Arabī*, p.542, no.783.

There are other works in regards to this issue.

due to the proofs of the servant's righteousness, closeness to good and the right way that this contains, and they maybe use this as a proof of the person's elevated status, position and virtue. Abū Bakr as-Siddīq ﷺ said: **"The best thing that any of you can see in a dream is to see His Lord or see His Prophet (ﷺ)."**[61]

As these reports had an effect on the soul of the one who reads them, we wanted to relay in this introductory theme a portion of these reports to motivate the concern for the soul and its rectification. Ibn Abī Ya'lā ﷺ in *Tabaqāt ul-Hanābilah*, vol.1, p.125 states:

> 'Ali informed us: from Ibn Battah who said: Abū Bakr al-Ājurrī narrated to us saying: I heard Ibn Abi't-Tayyib say: Ja'far as-Sā'igh narrated to me that a man who was a person who used to commit disobedience and immoralities was in the neighbourhood of Ahmad bin Hanbal. One day he came to the gathering of Ahmad bin Hanbal and gave salāms to him and it was as if Ahmad did not respond to him completely and refrained from him. The man said to him: "O Abū 'Abdullāh why do you turn away from me? For I have changed due to what I saw in a vision." Imām

---

[61] Reported by Ibn Abī 'Āsim in *as-Sunnah*, vol.1, p.215, no.488. Our Shaykh (i.e. al-Albānī, ﷺ said in *Dhilāl ul-Jannah*, vol.1, p.215: **"Its isnad is da'īf, the men in it are thiqāt except for al-'Abbās bin Maymūn who I do not know of."**

Ahmad then asked him: "What did you see? Come forward." The man said: "I saw the Prophet ﷺ while I was asleep and it was as if he was on highland while the people were sitting below him. Then a man got up and said to the Prophet: 'supplicate for me.' So he supplicated for him until there did not remain anyone left (asking for supplication) except for me. I wanted to stand to ask him but I remembered the filth that I used to do. Then the Prophet ﷺ said to me: 'O fulān, why did you not get up to ask me to supplicate for you?' I replied: 'O Messenger of Allāh, the shame is stopping me. It is due to the filth that I used to do.' Then the Prophet ﷺ said to me: 'If it is due to shame then stand and ask me to supplicate for you for indeed you are one who does not curse any of my Companions.' So I got up and he supplicated for me. [Since that dream] I paid attention to myself and Allāh made all that which I used to do to be disgusting to me." Then Abū 'Abdullāh said to us: "O Ja'far, O fulān, narrate this and preserve it, for it can bring benefit."

Of these narrations which can benefit include what was reported by Ibn Sa'd in *Tabaqāt ul-Kubrā*, vol.7, p.457 from 'AbdurRahmān bin Maysarah ؓ who said:

I saw the Prophet ﷺ in my sleep and I said to him: 'O Prophet of Allāh, supplicate for me so that I will

85

understand hadīth and be conscious of it.' He supplicated for me and (since that time) I do not hear anything except that I understand it.

Al-Hāfidh Ibn Hajar mentioned in *ad-Durar al-Kāminah*, vol.1, p.103 from Ahmad bin Ishāq bin Muhammad al-Hamadānī that he used to say: "I saw the Prophet ﷺ in a dream and he informed me that I will die in Makkah." He made Hajj towards the end of his life and died there.

As-Suyūtī ﷺ stated in *al-Araj ba'd al-Faraj*, p.61:

Ibn an-Najjār reported from al-Hasan bin Ahmad bin as-Saydalānī who said: my mother informed me that when she was pregnant: 'I asked Allāh to make it easy for me and in a dream I saw the Prophet ﷺ and he said to me: 'O beloved mother say: O Easer of hardships, O Softener of iron, O Fulfiller of promises and O You Who everyday creates a new matter – free me from this restriction to the vast path, *la hawla wa la quwwata ila billāh al-'Alī ul-Adhīm*."

In *Tabaqāt Ibn Sa'd*, vol.7, p.111 it is reported from Sa'īd al-Jarīrī ﷺ: A man saw Allāh's Messenger ﷺ in a dream and the man said to him: "O Allāh's Messenger seek forgiveness for me." Allāh's

Messenger replied: "Āmir seeks forgiveness for you."[62] The man said: "So I went to 'Āmir and told him and he shed tears, to the extent that I heard him whimper."

'Umar bin 'Abdul'Azīz ؓ said:

> "I saw the Prophet ﷺ in a dream and Banū Hāshim were requesting something for him. The Prophet ﷺ said to them: "Where is 'Umar bin 'Abdul'Azīz? (Request it from him)."[63]

A man came to 'Umar bin 'Abdul'Azīz once and said to him: I saw Allāh's Messenger ﷺ in a dream and Abū Bakr was on his right and 'Umar was on his left and you (O 'Umar bin 'Abdul'Azīz) were in front of Allāh's Messenger and he said to you: "O 'Umar, if you act then act by Abū Bakr and 'Umar." Then 'Umar bin 'Abdul'Azīz requested that the man swear that he saw such a vision saying: "By

---

[62] 'Āmir bin 'Abdillāh bin 'Abd Qays, the famous Tābi'ī.

[63] Reported by Ibn Sa'd in *at-Tabaqāt*, vol.3, p.291, vol.5, p.330; Abū Nu'aym, *al-Hilyah*, vol.5, p.336; Ibn Abi'd-Dunyā, *al-Manāmāt*, pp.119-120; via the route of transmission of Ibn 'Asākir in *Tārīkh Dimishq*, vol.45, pp.195-196; mentioned by adh-Dhahabī in *Siyar*, vol.5, p.127; Ibn ul-Jawzī, *Sīrat 'Umar bin 'Abdul'Azīz*, p.290; al-Malā', *Sīrah*, vol.5, p.526.

Allāh, did you really see this vision?" The man swore that he saw that and then 'Umar bin 'Abdul'Azīz burst into tears.[64]

Ismā'īl bin Yazīd ar-Raqī ﷺ stated:

A man from the Tābi'īn saw Allāh's Messenger ﷺ in a dream and said to him: 'O Allāh's Messenger admonish me.' He replied: 'Yes (I will).' And then he said to him: "Whoever intends deficiency has deficiency and whoever has deficiency then death is better for him."[65]

'AbdulGhanī an-Nāblusī transmitted from Ridwān bin Yūsuf, well-known as as-Sabbāgh, that he saw the Prophet ﷺ in a dream in the year 1102 AH in the 'Umarī Congregational Masjid and he saw the people crowded inside it and a man said: "O Ridwān!" And they both went inside the Masjid and saw Allāh's Messenger ﷺ who spoke to him and said 'O fulān (and mentioned his name): "Go and say from me: Live as you will for indeed you are to die, love whoever you will for indeed you will leave them and do as you will for indeed

---

[64] Reported by Ibn Sa'd in *at-Tabaqāt*, vol.3, p.291, vol.5, p.330; Imām Ahmad, *az-Zuhd*, pp.427-428, no.1697; Ibn Abi'd-Dunyā, *al-Manāmāt*, pp.119-120, 262; Ibn 'Asākir, *Tārīkh Dimishq*, vol.45, pp.246-247; mentioned by adh-Dhahabī in *Siyar A'lām un-Nubalā'*, vol.5, pp.127, 131; Ibn ul-Qayyim, *ar-Rūh*, p.41.

[65] Reported by Ibn Abi'd-Dunyā in *al-Manāmāt*, p.163, no.286 and p.179; also mentioned by al-Ghazālī in *al-Ihyā'* (Dār Tayyibah Print), vol.4, p.739.

you will be recompensed for it." The man left and conveyed just as the Prophet ﷺ mentioned.[66]

Ibrāhīm bin Ya'qūb ﷺ said:

A man of worship and virtue saw Allāh's Messenger ﷺ and said to him: "Seek forgiveness for me O Allāh's Messenger." The Messenger replied: "Turn away from me." I said to him: "O Allāh's Messenger! 'Sufyān ibn 'Uyaynah narrated to us: from Muhammad bin al-Munkadir from Jābir ibn 'Abdillāh that you were not asked of anything and said: 'no.' Then the Prophet ﷺ came close to me and said: 'May Allāh forgive you.'[67]

---

[66] Relayed from him by al-Murādī in *Silk ud-Durar* (Dār ul-'Ilmiyyah Print), vol.2, p.115.

Translator's note: the full title of Abu'l-Fadl Muhammad Khalīl al-Murādī's (d.1206 AH/1791 CE) above mentioned book is *Silk ud-Durar fi A'yān il-Qarn ith-Thānī 'Ashar* [String of Pearls: Eminent Persons of the Twelfth Century]. It was printed in four volumes by:

    ✓ Beirut: Dar Ibn Hazm, 1988

    ✓ Cairo: 1291-1301 AH/1874-1884 CE

    ✓ Baghdad: 1301 AH/1883-4 CE

    ✓ Cairo: Bulāq: 1291 AH

[67] Reported by Ibn Abi'd-Dunyā in *al-Manāmāt*, p.83, no.114 and also mentioned by al-Ghazālī in *al-Ihyā'* (Dār Tayyibah Print), vol.4, p.733

'AbdulWāhib bin Ādam at-Tawāwīsī ﷺ said:

I saw the Prophet ﷺ during sleep and he had a group of his companions with him and he was standing in a location. I gave salāms to him and he replied. I said: "Why are you standing here O Allāh's Messenger?" He replied: "I'm waiting for Muhammad bin Ismā'īl al-Bukhārī." Some days after this vision I was informed that al-Bukhārī had died and he died at the same time that I had seen the Prophet ﷺ in the vision.[68]

Al-Khatīb also reported in his *Tārīkh*, vol.2, p.10 with his chain of transmission from al-Farabrī[69] who said:

"I saw the Prophet ﷺ in a dream and he said to me: "Where do you want [to go]?" I replied: I want [to go to] Muhammad bin Ismā'īl al-Bukhārī." Then he said to me: "Convey my salāms to him."[70]

An-Najm bin al-Fudayl said:

---

[68] Reported by al-Khatīb, *Tārīkh Baghdād*, vol.2, p.34 and mentioned by adh-Dhahabī, *Siyar A'lām un-Nubalā'*, vol.12, p.468; Ibn ul-'Imād, *Shadharāt udh-Dhahab*, vol.2, p.135.

[69] [TN] Abū 'Abdullāh Muhammad ibn Yūsuf ibn Mitr ibn Sālih ibn Bishr ibn Ibrāhīm al-Farabrī (d. 320 AH/932 CE).

[70] *Siyar A'lām*, vol.12, p.443 and *Hadī's-Sārī* (Dār ul-Fikr Print), p.677

I saw the Prophet ﷺ in a dream and it was as if he was walking and Muhammad bin Ismāʿīl [al-Bukhārī] was walking behind him. Whenever the Prophet ﷺ raised his foot, Muhammad bin Ismāʿīl al-Bukhārī would place his foot in that place.[71]

The likes of this have also been reported about our Shaykh, al-Albānī ﷺ, when an Algerian woman saw him walking behind the Prophet ﷺ and he was placing his feet in the places where the Prophet ﷺ placed his.[72] There is no doubt this dream was of the glad-tidings which indicate his virtue and safeguarding of the Sunnah and his *daʿwah* unto it for which he became known and famed for. Such a dream does not need much interpretation, all praise is due to Allāh, the interpretation is clear without the slightest bit of burden to interpret it.

ʾAbdullāh ibn ʾAwn ﷺ, the noble Tābiʾī said:

---

[71] Reported by al-Khatīb in *Tārīkh Baghdād*, vol.2, p.10; al-Harawī in *Dhamm ul-Kalām*, vol.2, p.271, no.347; *Siyar Aʿlām un-Nubalāʾ*, vol.12, p.405 and *Hadīʾs-Sārī*, p.677.

[72] As is mentioned in audio cassette no.50 of *Silsilat ul-Hudā waʾn-Nūr*, the Shaykh burst into tears upon hearing about this vision as did those present in the gathering from the Shaykh's beloved companions, students and followers.

I saw in a dream that I was with Muhammad in a garden and was walking with him, he passed by a stream which he fixed and I was behind him so I did just as he did...[73]

Abū Zayd al-Marwazī al-Faqīh ﷻ said:

I was sleeping between the *Rukn* and the *Maqām* and I saw the Prophet ﷺ and he said to me: "O Abū Zayd, up until when will you teach the book of ash-Shāfi'ī and not teach my book?" I said to him: "O Allāh's Messenger, and what is your book?" He replied: "The Jāmi' of Muhammad ibn Ismā'īl (al-Bukhārī)."[74]

A dream of this type was also affirmed in regards to our Shaykh, al-Albānī ﷻ: our noble brother 'Izzat Khadr *(hafidhahullāh)* narrated to us saying:

A common man in Shām saw Allāh's Messenger ﷺ in a dream and said to him: "O Allāh's Messenger teach me how to pray like your prayer." The Messenger replied: "If you

---

[73] Reported by Ibn Sa'd, *at-Tabaqāt al-Kubrā*, vol.7, p.265 – via Ibn 'Asākir in *Tārīkh Dimishq* (Dār ul-Fikr), vol.31, p.365.

[74] Reported by al-Harawī in *Dhamm ul-Kalām*, vol.2, pp.271-272, no.348; ar-Rāfi'ī, *at-Tadwīn*, vol.2, p.46; mentioned by adh-Dhahabī in *as-Siyar*, vol.12, p.438; Ibn Muflih, *Masā'ib ul-Insān*, p.176; Ibn Hajar, *Hadī's-Sārī* (Dār ul-Fikr Print), p.677; al-Qāsimī, *al-Fadl ul-Mubīn*, p.124.

want to pray like my prayer then read the book *Sifat us-Salāh an-Nabī Ka'annaka Tarāhā* [A Description of the Prophet's Prayer Described as if you are Seeing it] by Muhammad Nāsiruddīn al-Albānī.' The man awoke and memorised the name of the book and the author and the man had never heard the names before that.[75]

This dream also resembles what was also narrated to us by Abū 'Abdullāh 'Izzat Khadr *(hafidhahullāh)* that one day he was in a Taxi and he had a load of books and notes with him... an old man started to ask him questions about the book *Ahkām ul-Janā'iz* by al-Albānī ﷺ. He read the title as it was the first book within brother 'Izzat's bag, when brother 'Izzat saw the man's intense want for the book he gave it to the man as a gift. The man then said to brother 'Izzat:

> I was called today to wash the body of a dead person from my relatives. I was the eldest so the family requested that I wash the body as is natural. I did not wash the body properly and I finished it quickly and then he was buried on the same day. When I went home at the end of the day I slept and I saw my dead relative in a dream and he was angry with me saying: "You did not wash me properly." I

---

[75] This was one of many visions which affected the Shaykh *(rahimahullāh)* and led him to shed tears.

replied: "I did not know how to wash the body of a dead person." My relative then said to me: "Read the book *Ahkām ul-Janā'iz* by Shaykh Muhammad Nāsiruddīn al-Albānī."

Then the man woke up from his sleep and memorised the name of the book and the author, and a few days later the brother 'Izzat Khadr gave him the book. Glory be to Allāh for how truthful this vision is for the advice and guidance that it contains and your amazement would possibly increase if you were to know that the man who saw the vision had never heard of the book or the author before that, however it was of the blessings and subtleties of Allāh towards his servants – all praise is due to Allāh.[76] We do not rely on dreams in order to show the Shaykh's virtue ﷺ but they are from a believer's glad-tidings especially if they occur often. Of these natural emotive dreams is what was mentioned by al-Hāfidh Ibn Hajar in *ad-Durur al-Kāminah*, vol.1, p.376 in the biography of Ismā'īl bin

---

[76] This dream in regards to the virtue of the Shaykh was mentioned in front of a group of his students, one of them said, who was the brother Husayn al-'Awā'ishah (*hafidhahullāh*):

"When this dream about Imām al-Albānī ﷺ was mentioned he cried and said: 'If the report of this dream reached me before the book was printed I would have mentioned it in the book's introduction.'"

For other dreams regarding our Shaykh al-Albānī ﷺ refer to our journal *al-Asālah*, no.23, 15 Sha'bān 1420 AH, pp.26-27.

Sa'īd al-Kurdī al-Misrī who was accused of *Zandaqah* (heresy) and *kufr* (disbelief) so Taqiuddīn al-Akhnā'ī called for him, so he was summoned but was confusing in his speech and thus subsequently imprisoned. Al-Hāfidh said:

> A pious man came and informed that he saw the Prophet ﷺ in a dream who said to him: "Tell al-Akhnā'ī to strike the neck of Ismā'īl for he curses my brother Lūt." So Ismā'īl was summoned again and a gathering was arranged, the proof was established on him and then it was instructed to execute him.

It was mentioned in the biography of Ahmad bin al-Hasan ar-Rāzī that when he got older his back bent and when he was sick he would say: "Allāh's Messenger informed me in a dream that I would live long."[77] Al-Hasan bin Qāsim al-Murādī ﷺ stated:

> "I saw the Prophet ﷺ in a dream and he said to me: 'O Hasan! Sit and benefit the people at the place of the Mihrāb in the old Jāmi' (congregational masjid) of Misr.'"[78]

Muhammad bin Fadālah said:

---

[77] Mentioned by al-Hāfidh in *ad-Durar*, vol.1, p.118, no.328 and then he said: **"This is what occurred for he lived for over ninety years."**

[78] Mentioned by al-Hāfidh in *ad-Durar al-Kāminah*, vol.2, p.32, no.1546

I saw the Prophet *(sallallāhu 'alayhi wassallam)* in a dream and he said to us: "Visit 'Abdullāh ibn 'Awn for Allāh and His Messenger love him and he loves Allāh and His Messenger."[79]

In the reports of Abū 'Ubayd bin al-Qāsim ibn Sallām it is mentioned that he wanted to depart for al-'Irāq in order to seek knowledge and earn a living, he said:

> I saw Allāh's Messenger ﷺ in a dream and I wanted to go to visit him yet I was prevented from doing so. It was said to me: "Do not go to visit him and do not give salāms while you are going to al-'Irāq." I replied: "I will not go at all then." They then took a promise from me on this, then I saw him and I gave him salāms and he shook my hand.[80]

Muhammad bin Nasr at-Tūsī ﷺ said:

> I saw the Prophet ﷺ in a dream and I said to him: "Instruct me with something that I may adhere to." He said: "Have certainty."[81]

---

[79] Reported by Ibn 'Asākir ﷺ in *Tārīkh Dimishq*, vol.31, p.366.

[80] Reported by Ibn Sa'd in *at-Tabaqāt*, vol.7, pp.268-269; Ibn 'Adiyy, *al-Kāmil*, vol.6, pp.169-170; al-Mizzī, *Tahdhīb ul-Kamāl*, vol.17, pp.147-148.

[81] The report is found in *Siyar A'lām un-Nubalā'*, vol.12, p.213

Adh-Dhahabī mentions in *Siyar A'lām un-Nubalā'*, vol.14, p.38 from Imām Muhammad bin Nasr al-Marwazī that he said:

I did not have a good opinion of ash-Shāfi'ī and on one day when I was sitting in the Prophet's Masjid I fell asleep and saw the Prophet ﷺ in a dream and I said to him: "O Messenger of Allāh should I write down the opinions of ash-Shāfi'ī?" The Prophet ﷺ shook his head out of anger and said: "You call it 'opinion' it is not mere 'opinion' it is a response to those who oppose my Sunnah." I went to Egypt affected by this vision and I wrote out the books of ash-Shāfi'ī.

Al-Khatīb ﷺ said in *Mas'alat ul-Ihtijāj bi'sh-Shāfi'ī*, p.125:

Abu'l-Qāsim Hibatullāh bin al-Hasan bin Mansūr narrated to me saying: I saw Allāh's Messenger ﷺ in a dream and I said to him: "O Allāh's Messenger what do you say about Sahīh ul-Bukhārī?" The Messenger said to me: "All of it is Sahīh!" Or 'all of it is "good" or the likes of this...[82]

---

[82] Al-Bukhārī did not report from ash-Shāfi'ī even though they lived at the same time, al-Bukhārī did not meet him for he (al-Bukhārī) was young even though he met those older than ash-Shāfi'ī and had higher narrations. If he did report from him it would have been via another in between them. Refer to Abū Zu'rah al-'Irāqī in *Ajwibat ul-Mardiyyah 'an As'ilat al-Makkiyyah*, p.110.

Harmalah ﷺ said:

I heard ash-Shāfi'ī ﷺ say: when I was young in Makkah I saw in a dream a man of prestige leading the people in Masjid ul-Harām and when he finished his prayer he went to the people and began teaching them. I got close to him and I said to the man: "Teach me." The man then produced some scales from his sleeve and gave them to me saying: "These are for you." I went to a dream interpreter with this and he said to me: "you will reach the level of, and become, an Imām in knowledge and you will be on the right path and on the Sunnah, because the Imām of Masjid ul-Harām is the best of all Imāms and the highest of them. As for the scales then you will teach the reality of things in themselves."[83]

---

[83] Reported by al-Bayhaqī ﷺ in *Manāqib ush-Shāfi'ī*, vol.1, pp.98-99; ar-Rāzī, *Manāqib ush-Shāfi'ī*, pp.36-37; mentioned by Ibn Hajar in *Tuwālī ut-Ta'nīs*, p.52.

NOTES

NOTES